UNBROKEN

Abigail Tandoh Norman
Unbroken

All rights reserved
Copyright © 2024 by Abigail Tandoh Norman

No part of this publication may be reproduced, distributed, or transmitted in any form or by any means, including photocopying, recording, or other electronic or mechanical methods, without the prior written permission of the publisher, except in the case of brief quotations embodied in critical reviews and certain other noncommercial uses permitted by copyright law.

Published by BooxAI
ISBN: 978-965-578-816-7

UNBROKEN

A JOURNEY OF "HEALING, HOPE, AND WHOLENESS FOR THE SINGLE, DIVORCED, AND BROKEN"

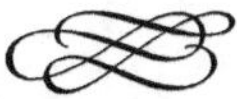

ABIGAIL TANDOH NORMAN

CONTENTS

ACKNOWLEDGMENTS

I would like to express my deepest gratitude and heartfelt acknowledgment for this book. This book is a testament to my journey with God and the incredible transformation that has taken place in my life.

First and foremost, I want to thank God for His unwavering love, grace, and guidance throughout my healing journey. It is through His divine intervention and constant presence that I have been able to navigate through the challenges and trials that came my way. His faithfulness has brought me to a place of maturity and deepened my relationship with Him.

I would like to extend my gratitude to my whole family, especially my mom, daughter, and brother. They have been a supportive system during the most difficult moments of my life. Their love, encouragement, and prayers have uplifted me and helped me persevere. My husband for being supportive and encouraging in all areas of my life. I am blessed to have such incredible family members who have stood by me through thick and thin.

Lastly, I want to give credit and thanks to my late father, "Apostle James Asankoma-Tandoh." He had been the pillar and mentor of our faith and Christian walk. His unwavering belief in God and his teachings have shaped my understanding of spirituality and guided me on this journey. I am forever grateful for his guidance, wisdom, and love.

In conclusion, I am humbled and grateful for the experiences and people that have shaped my journey with God. This book is a testament to His faithfulness and the transformative power of His love. May it inspire and encourage others on their own spiritual and healing journeys. All glory and honor belong to God alone.

INTRODUCTION

A new year Declaration

As we enter into a new year, let us declare and affirm the following truths based on God's Word:

1. "I declare that this year is a year of new beginnings and fresh opportunities. God is doing a new thing in my life." (Isaiah 43:19)

2. "I affirm that God's plans for me are good and full of hope. He has a purpose for my life, and I will walk in His divine destiny." (Jeremiah 29:11)

3. "I declare that I am a child of God, and I am deeply loved and cherished by Him. His love for me is unchanging and everlasting." (Romans 8:38-39)

4. "I affirm that I am more than a conqueror through Christ who strengthens me. I will overcome every obstacle and walk in victory." (Romans 8:37)

5. "I declare that God's grace is sufficient for me. His power is made perfect in my weakness, and I will rely on His strength." (2 Corinthians 12:9)

6. "I affirm that I am a vessel of God's peace. His peace will guard my heart and mind, even in the midst of challenges." (Philippians 4:7)

7. "I declare that I will trust in the Lord with all my heart and lean not on my own understanding. He will direct my paths." (Proverbs 3:5-6)

8. "I affirm that I am a light in the world. I will shine God's love and truth to those around me, making a difference in their lives." (Matthew 5:14)

9. "I declare that I will seek first the kingdom of God and His righteousness. He will provide for all my needs." (Matthew 6:33)

10. "I affirm that I am a disciple of Christ. I will follow Him wholeheartedly and grow in my relationship with Him." (John 8:31)

11. "I declare that I will not be anxious about anything, but in everything, I will present my requests to God with thanksgiving. His peace will guard my heart and mind." (Philippians 4:6-7)

12. "I affirm that I am a vessel of God's love. His love will flow through me, touching the lives of those around me." (1 John 4:7)

13. "I declare that I will walk in integrity and righteousness. I will honor God in all that I do and be a

reflection of His character." (Proverbs 11:3)

14. "I affirm that I am a chosen instrument of God. He has appointed me to bear fruit that will last and make an impact for His kingdom." (John 15:16)

15. "I declare that I will not be conformed to the patterns of this world, but I will be transformed by the renewing of my mind. I will align my thoughts with God's truth." (Romans 12:2)

16. "I affirm that I am a vessel of God's joy. His joy will be my strength, and I will rejoice in Him always." (Nehemiah 8:10)

17. "I declare that I will walk in humility and serve others with love. I will follow the example of Jesus, who came to serve." (Mark 10:45)

18. "I affirm that I am a temple of the Holy Spirit. God's Spirit dwells within me, empowering and guiding me." (1 Corinthians 6:19)

19. "I declare that I will be diligent and faithful in all that I do. I will work as unto the Lord, knowing that my labor is not in vain." (Colossians 3:23-24)

20. "I affirm that I am a witness of God's love and truth. I will share the good news of Jesus Christ with others, pointing them to Him." (Acts 1:8)

May these affirmations and declarations guide us throughout the year, reminding us of who we are in Christ and the promises we have in Him. Let us trust in His faithfulness and walk in His truth. Amen.

COMPLETE IN HIM

Day 1: "I affirm that God's love for me is unchanging, regardless of my relationship status. I trust in His perfect plan for my life." (Romans 8:38-39)

Prayer

Dear Heavenly Father,

Thank you for your unchanging love and perfect plan for my life. I know that my worth is not determined by my relationship status. Help me to remember that I am fearfully and wonderfully made and that my value comes from you. Give me the strength to trust in your timing and to focus on growing my relationship with you. Guide me in embracing my uniqueness and celebrating my heritage. Fill my heart with confidence and joy, knowing that I am a beautiful creation.

Thank you for your love and plans for my life. May your will be done.

In Jesus' name, I pray.

Amen.

Day 2: "I affirm that I am complete in Christ, and my worth is not defined by my marital status. I embrace my singleness as an opportunity for growth and service." (Colossians 2:10)

Prayer

Dear Heavenly Father,

Thank you for the completeness I find in you. Help me to embrace my singleness as an opportunity for growth and service. Guide me in using this season to draw closer to you and make a difference in the lives of others. Give me the strength to resist societal pressures and trust in your perfect timing. Fill my heart with contentment and peace, knowing that I am complete in you. Thank you for your unconditional love and the plan you have for my life. May your will be done as I continue to grow in my faith and service to you.

In Jesus' name, I pray.

Amen.

Day 3: "I affirm that God's grace is sufficient for me in every season of life. I lean on His strength to navigate the challenges of being single or divorced." (2 Corinthians 12:9)

Prayer

Dear Heavenly Father,

Thank you for your abundant grace and strength that sustains me in every season of life. Whether I am single or divorced, I know that your grace is sufficient for me. Help me to remember that I am never alone and to find solace in your presence. Guide me in embracing my singleness or divorce as an opportunity for growth and healing. Teach me to find joy and contentment in my relationship with you and to use my experiences to encourage and uplift others. Thank you for your unfailing love and grace. May your grace continue to guide me in every season of life.

In Jesus' name, I pray.

Amen.

Day 4: "I affirm that God is my ultimate source of joy and fulfillment. I find contentment in His presence, knowing that He satisfies the deepest longings of my heart." (Psalm 16:11)

Prayer

Dear Heavenly Father,

Thank you for the joy and fulfillment I find in your presence. Remind me that true joy can only be found in you. Help me seek you above all else and find contentment in your unfailing love. Guide me in cultivating a deeper relationship with you and experiencing the fullness of your joy. Teach me to trust in your plans and find peace in your presence. Thank you for filling my life with joy, and may I always find contentment in you.

In Jesus' name, I pray.

Amen.

Day 5: "I affirm that God has a purpose for my singleness or divorce. I surrender my desires and plans to Him, trusting that He will guide me towards His perfect will." (Proverbs 3:5-6)

Prayer

Father, in the name of Jesus, I surrender my singleness or divorce to you, knowing that you have a purpose and plan for my life. Help me to trust in you and lean not on my own understanding. Guide me in every decision and step I take. Give me the wisdom to recognize your guidance and the courage to follow it. Remind me of your faithfulness and love in moments of doubt. Strengthen my faith and help me to wait patiently for your perfect timing.

Thank you for your guidance and provision. May your will be done in my life.

In Jesus' name, I pray.

Amen.

Day 6: "I affirm that God's love heals all wounds. I release any bitterness or resentment from past relationships, allowing His love to restore and renew my heart." (Psalm 147:3)

Prayer

Father, in the name of Jesus, I come before you with a broken heart, seeking your healing touch. Please mend the broken pieces and restore my heart. I release any bitterness or unforgiveness and ask for your grace to forgive those who have hurt me. Fill my heart with your perfect and unconditional love, removing any barriers or walls I have built. Guide me in choosing healthy and loving relationships, and teach me to love others as you love me. Thank you for your promise to heal the brokenhearted. I trust in your faithfulness to restore and renew my heart. May your love flow through me and touch the lives of those around me.

In Jesus' name, I pray.

Amen.

Day 7: "I affirm that God is my refuge and strength in times of loneliness or heartache. I find comfort in His presence and trust in His faithfulness." (Psalm 46:1)

Prayer

Father, in the name of Jesus, I find comfort in your presence and trust in your faithfulness. Remind me that I am never alone, for you are always by my side. Help me to find solace in your presence and trust in your plan for my life. In times of heartache, I lean on your strength and find refuge in you. Help me to surrender my pain to you, knowing that you can bring beauty from ashes. Thank you for being my refuge and strength. May your love and peace fill my heart, even in times of loneliness or heartache. Guide and strengthen me, and may I always find my refuge in you.

In Jesus' name, I pray.

Amen.

Day 8: "I affirm that God's timing is perfect. I trust in His plan for my future and believe that He will bring the right person into my life at the right time." (Ecclesiastes 3:11)

Prayer

Heavenly Father,

I trust in your perfect timing and plan for my future. Help me to be patient and have faith, knowing that you will bring the right person into my life at the right time. Guide me in preparing myself for that future relationship and help me to grow in my relationship with you. Teach me to love others as you love me. Thank you for your perfect timing and for always being in control. May your will be done in my life.

In Jesus' name, I pray.

Amen.

Day 9: "I affirm that God's love for me is unconditional. I am worthy of love and respect, and I will not settle for anything less than His best for me." (1 John 4:10)

Prayer

Father, in the name of Jesus, Thank you for your unconditional love and for affirming my worth. Help me to embrace this truth and not settle for anything less than your best for me. Remind me of your love in moments of doubt or insecurity. Guide me in seeking your best, and give me the patience to wait for your perfect timing. I surrender my desires and plans to you, knowing that you have a perfect plan for my life. Fill my heart with your love and help me to always seek your best.

In Jesus' name, I pray.

Amen.

Day 10: "I affirm that God is my provider. He meets all my needs, and I trust Him to provide for me financially, emotionally, and spiritually." (Philippians 4:19)

Prayer

Heavenly Father,

I believe you to be my provider, and I trust in your promise to meet all my needs. I surrender my financial worries to you, trusting that you will provide for me and help me manage my resources wisely. I also surrender my emotional needs to you, knowing that you are the God of all comfort and will bring healing and peace. Lastly, I surrender my spiritual needs to you, seeking your guidance and nourishment for my soul. Thank you for being my provider, and may your provision bring glory to your name.

In Jesus' name, I pray.

Amen.

Day 11: "I affirm that God's peace surpasses all understanding. I choose to cast my anxieties on Him and find rest in His presence." (Philippians 4:6-7)

Prayer

Father, in the name of Jesus, I surrender my anxieties and worries to you, finding rest in your presence. Fill me with your peace that surpasses all understanding. Help me to trust in your provision and guidance, letting go of control.

Remind me of your faithfulness in moments of fear or uncertainty. Give me strength and courage to face each day with confidence, knowing you are with me. Thank you for the peace that fills my heart and mind. May I always trust in your provision and guidance.

In Jesus' name, I pray.

Amen.

Day 12: "I affirm that God's Word is a lamp to my feet and a light to my path. I seek His guidance and wisdom in all areas of my life, including relationships." (Psalm 119:105)

Prayer

Heavenly Father,

I surrender my relationships to you and seek your guidance and wisdom. Help me choose the right people to surround myself with and build healthy, God-honoring relationships. Give me the strength to let go of any relationships not aligned with your will. Guide me in my current relationships, teaching me effective communication, understanding, and love. Help me deepen my relationship with you and love others as you love me. Fill me with your Holy Spirit, and may my relationships reflect your love and grace.

In Jesus' name, I pray.

Amen.

Day 13: "I affirm that God's love for me is everlasting. I am secure in His love, and I will not be swayed by the opinions or actions of others." (Jeremiah 31:3)

Prayer

Father, in the name of Jesus, thank you for your everlasting love. Help me find my worth and security in your love alone, not in the opinions of others. Remind me of your unfailing love in moments of doubt or insecurity. Give me the strength to stand firm in your love, even when faced with rejection or criticism. Fill my heart with your love and guide my steps. May I always find my worth and security in you alone.

In Jesus' name, I pray.

Amen.

Day 14: "I affirm that God's grace is sufficient for me. I am forgiven and set free from my past mistakes, and I choose to extend grace and forgiveness to others." (2 Corinthians 12:9)

Prayer

Heavenly Father, I acknowledge that your grace is sufficient for me. I am grateful for the forgiveness and freedom I have through Jesus Christ. Help me extend grace and forgiveness to others, letting go of grudges and choosing love. Fill my heart with your love and compassion. Remind me of your grace in moments of weakness, and give me the courage to forgive others.

Thank you for your abundant grace. May it transform my heart and guide my actions. May I always reflect your love and grace to others.

In Jesus' name, I pray.

Amen.

Day 15: "I affirm that God is my strength and my song. I will praise Him in every season of life, knowing that He is with me and will never leave me." (Exodus 15:2)

Prayer

Heavenly Father,

You are my strength and my song. I will praise you in every season of life, knowing that you are with me. I surrender my weaknesses and insecurities to you, trusting in your strength to carry me through. Help me rely on your power, knowing you can do more than I can imagine. I also surrender my joys and victories to you, giving you all the glory. Help me have a grateful heart and offer songs of praise to you. In every season, I choose to praise you, trusting that you are working all things for my good. Thank you for being my strength and my song.

In Jesus' name, I pray.

Amen.

Day 16: "I affirm that God's plans for me are good. I trust in His sovereignty and believe that He is working all things together for my good." (Jeremiah 29:11)

Prayer

Heavenly Father,

I trust in your good plans for me and believe that you are working all things together for my good. Help me to trust in your goodness and surrender my own plans to you. Give me strength to align my will with yours and to walk in obedience to your leading. I surrender my fears and worries to you, trusting in your sovereignty and control over every situation. In every circumstance, I choose to trust in your plans and believe that you are working all things together for my good. Thank you for your faithfulness and goodness.

In Jesus' name, I pray.

Amen.

Day 17: "I affirm that God's love for me is unfailing. I am deeply loved and cherished by Him, and I will not settle for anything less than His best for me." (Psalm 136:26)

Prayer

Heavenly Father,

I affirm your unfailing love for me. Help me fully embrace and receive your love. Fill me with the understanding that I am valued and cherished by you. Teach me to see myself as your beloved child. Give me confidence and security in your love. Remind me of your love in moments of doubt or insecurity. Help me reject lies that diminish my worth. Give me strength to stand firm in your love and seek your best for my life. Thank you for your unfailing love. May it transform my heart and guide my steps. May I always walk in the truth of your love.

In Jesus' name, I pray.

Amen.

Day 18: "I affirm that God's strength is made perfect in my weakness. I rely on His strength to overcome any challenges or struggles I may face." (2 Corinthians 12:9)

Prayer

Heavenly Father,

I acknowledge my weakness and surrender it to you. I rely on your strength to overcome challenges and struggles. Help me trust in your provision and guidance. Give me the courage to step out in faith. Remind me of your strength in moments of doubt. Fill me with your Holy Spirit to overcome obstacles. Thank you for your perfect strength. Guide and empower me to walk in your strength each day.

In Jesus' name, I pray.

Amen.

Day 19: "I affirm that God's love for me is unchanging. I am secure in His love, and I will not be swayed by the opinions or actions of others." (Romans 8:38-39)

Prayer

Heavenly Father,

I affirm your unchanging love for me. Help me find my worth and security in your love alone. Teach me to rely on your unfailing love, even in the face of rejection or criticism. Give me strength to stand firm in your love, knowing I am cherished and valued by you. Remind me of your love in moments of doubt or insecurity. Fill my heart with your love and assurance that I may walk in confidence and security. Thank you for your unchanging love. May it transform my heart and guide my steps. May I always find my worth and security in you alone.

In Jesus' name, I pray.

Amen.

Day 20: "I affirm that God is my comforter in times of loneliness or heartache. I find solace in His presence and trust in His faithfulness." (Psalm 34:18)

Prayer

Heavenly Father,

You are my comforter in times of loneliness and heartache. I find solace in your presence and trust in your faithfulness. Help me turn to you for comfort and find rest in your arms. I surrender my pain and sorrow to you, trusting that you are working all things together for my good. Give me the strength to lean on you and find comfort in your promises. Thank you for being my ever-present help in times of trouble. May your comfort and peace surround me always.

In Jesus' name, I pray.

Amen.

Day 21: "I affirm that God's love for me is unconditional. I am worthy of love and respect, and I will not settle for anything less than His best for me." (1 John 4:10

Prayer

Heavenly Father,

I affirm your unconditional love for me. Help me embrace and receive your love. Fill me with the understanding that I am valued and cherished by you. Teach me to see myself as your beloved child. Help me walk in confidence and security, knowing I am worthy of your love. Remind me of your love in moments of doubt. Give me the strength to reject lies that diminish my worth. Thank you for your unconditional love. May it transform my heart and guide my steps. May I always walk in the truth that I am worthy of your best for me.

In Jesus' name, I pray.

Amen.

Day 22: "I affirm that God's peace surpasses all understanding. I choose to cast my anxieties on Him and find rest in His presence." (Philippians 4:6-7)

Prayer

Heavenly Father,

I affirm that your peace surpasses all understanding. I surrender my worries and fears to you, knowing that you are in control and care for me. Help me find peace in your presence. Fill me with your calming presence and help me trust in your faithfulness. Give me strength to release my burdens to you. I choose to trust in your promises and find rest in your presence. Help me let go of anxieties and fully rely on you. Give me the peace that surpasses all understanding. Thank you for your peace. May it guard my heart and mind, and may I always trust in your faithfulness.

In Jesus' name, I pray.

Amen.

Day 23: "I affirm that God's Word is a lamp to my feet and a light to my path. I seek His guidance and wisdom in all areas of my life, including relationships." (Psalm 119:105)

Prayer

Heavenly Father,

I surrender my relationship to you. Guide me in seeking your wisdom and discernment. Help me recognize healthy and godly relationships, and give me the courage to let go of any that are not aligned with your will. Teach me to love others as you love me, treating them with kindness, respect, and forgiveness. Give me wisdom in choosing the right people to surround myself with, and help me build relationships rooted in love, trust, and mutual edification. Help me set healthy boundaries and communicate effectively. May my relationships reflect your love and grace, and may I be a source of encouragement and support to others.

In Jesus' name, I pray.

Amen.

Day 24: "I affirm that God's love for me is everlasting. I am secure in His love, and I will not be swayed by the opinions or actions of others." (Jeremiah 31:3)

Prayer

Heavenly Father,

I affirm your everlasting love for me. Help me embrace and receive your unchanging love. Teach me to find my worth and security in your love alone. Give me confidence and assurance in knowing that I am deeply loved by you. Remind me of your love in moments of doubt or insecurity. Help me reject negative thoughts and stand firm in your love. Thank you for your everlasting love. May it transform my heart and guide my steps.

May I always find my worth and security in you alone.

In Jesus' name, I pray.

Amen.

Day 25: "I affirm that God's grace is sufficient for me. I am forgiven and set free from my past mistakes, and I choose to extend grace and forgiveness to others." (2 Corinthians 12:9)

Prayer

Heavenly Father,

Your grace is sufficient for me. I am forgiven and set free from my past mistakes. Help me embrace and receive your grace. Teach me to walk in the freedom and forgiveness you have given me. Give me a heart that is quick to forgive and release any bitterness or resentment. Thank you for your abundant grace. May it transform my heart and guide my actions. Help me extend grace and forgiveness to others, just as you have extended it to me.

In Jesus' name, I pray.

Amen.

Day 26: "I affirm that God is my strength and my song. I will praise Him in every season of life, knowing that He is with me and will never leave me." (Exodus 15:2)

Prayer

Heavenly Father,

You are my strength and my song. I surrender my weaknesses and limitations to you, knowing that I can do all things through you who strengthens me. Help me rely on your strength and power. In difficult moments, help me praise you and have a heart of gratitude. Help me see your hand at work and trust in your faithfulness. Thank you for being my strength and my song. May my life reflect your goodness and grace. May I always find my strength and joy in you.

In Jesus' name, I pray.

Amen.

Day 27: "I affirm that God's plans for me are good. I trust in His sovereignty and believe that He is working all things together for my good." (Jeremiah 29:11)

Prayer

Heavenly Father,

I trust in your good plans for me. Help me to have faith in your sovereignty and purpose for my life. Guide me in surrendering my desires and aligning my heart with your will. I believe that you are working all things together for my good, even when I can't see the bigger picture. Thank you for your faithfulness and goodness. May I always seek your will and trust in your guidance. May my life reflect your grace and goodness.

In Jesus' name, I pray.

Amen.

Day 28: "I affirm that God's love for me is unfailing. I am deeply loved and cherished by Him, and I will not settle for anything less than His best for me." (Psalm 136:26)

Prayer

Heavenly Father,

Your love for me is unfailing. Help me understand and believe in your love. Fill me with the understanding that I am your beloved child and that you have a plan for my life. Teach me to walk in confidence, knowing I am deeply loved by you.

Remind me of your love in moments of doubt. Help me reject thoughts that diminish my worth. Give me strength to stand firm in your love and trust in your faithfulness.

Thank you for your unfailing love. May it transform my heart and guide my steps. Help me never settle for anything less than your best for me.

In Jesus' name, I pray.

Amen.

Day 29: "I affirm that God's strength is made perfect in my weakness. I rely on His strength to overcome any challenges or struggles I may face." (2 Corinthians 12:9)

Prayer

Heavenly Father,

I rely on your strength to overcome challenges and struggles. I surrender my weaknesses to you, knowing that I can do all things through you who strengthen me. Help me trust in your faithfulness and walk in confidence, knowing you are with me. Thank you for your perfect strength. May it sustain me and guide my steps. Help me walk in victory, knowing you are always with me.

In Jesus' name, I pray.

Amen.

Day 30: "I affirm that God's love for me is unchanging. I am secure in His love, and I will not be swayed by the opinions or actions of others." (Romans 8:38-39)

Prayer

Heavenly Father,

I affirm that your love for me is unchanging. Help me fully embrace and receive your constant and unwavering love. Teach me to find my worth and security in your love alone. Remind me of your unchanging love in moments of doubt or insecurity. Give me the strength to stand firm in your love and reject negative thoughts. Thank you for your unchanging love. May it transform my heart and guide my steps. May I always find my worth and security in you alone.

In Jesus' name, I pray.

Amen.

Day 31: "I affirm that God is my comforter in times of loneliness or heartache. I find solace in His presence and trust in His faithfulness." (Psalm 34:18)

Prayer

Heavenly Father,

You are my comforter in times of loneliness and heartache. I surrender my feelings to you and trust in your faithfulness. Help me find solace in your presence and lean on you for support. Remind me of your love and give me strength to endure. Thank you for being my comforter. May your love and comfort bring healing and restoration. I find my refuge in you.

In Jesus' name, I pray.

Amen.

HE WILL SEE ME THROUGH

Day 1: "I affirm that God is my refuge and strength, a very present help in times of trouble. I find comfort and strength in His presence, knowing that He will never leave me nor forsake me." (Psalm 46:1)

Prayer

Heavenly Father,

You are my refuge and strength, always present in times of trouble. I surrender my burdens to you and trust in your faithfulness. Help me find solace in your presence and lean on you for support. Remind me of your unfailing love, and give me peace and strength. Thank you for being my refuge and strength. May your love and peace surround me always.

In Jesus' name, I pray.

Amen.

Day 2: "I affirm that God is faithful, even when others may betray or disappoint me. I trust in His unfailing love and His plans for my life." (Psalm 36:5)

Prayer

Heavenly Father,

I affirm your faithfulness, even in the face of betrayal or disappointment. Help me trust in your unfailing love and plans for my life. Remind me that you are always with me, even in difficult times. Teach me to find security and hope in you alone. Give me the strength to forgive and trust in your plans, even when they differ from my own. Thank you for your faithfulness. May it guide me and give me hope. May I always find peace and security in you.

In Jesus' name, I pray.

Amen.

Day 3: "I affirm that God is my healer. He binds up the brokenhearted and brings restoration and healing to my wounded soul." (Psalm 147:3)

Prayer

Heavenly Father,

You are my healer. I surrender my brokenness and pain to you. Please bring restoration and healing to my wounded soul. Help me let go of bitterness and resentment. Fill me with your love and peace. Remind me of your healing presence in times of despair. Grant me strength to walk through the healing process, knowing you are with me. Thank you for being my healer. May your touch bring wholeness and peace to my life. In Jesus' name, I pray.

Amen.

Day 4: "I affirm that God is my provider. He meets all my needs according to His riches in glory, and He will never leave me lacking." (Philippians 4:19)

Prayer

Heavenly Father,

You are my provider. I surrender my worries and anxieties about provision to you. I trust in your faithfulness and provision in every area of my life. Help me rely on your provision and not my own efforts. Remind me of your promise to provide for me in times of uncertainty. Give me wisdom to steward the resources you have given me. Thank you for being my provider. May I always find security and sufficiency in you. May your provision flow abundantly in my life, bringing glory to your name.

In Jesus' name, I pray.

Amen.

Day 5: "I affirm that God is my strength and my shield. He gives me the strength to persevere through difficult times and protects me from harm." (Psalm 28:7)

Prayer

Heavenly Father,

You are my strength and shield. I surrender my weaknesses and vulnerabilities to you. Please give me the strength to overcome challenges and protect me from harm. Help me rely on your strength, not my own abilities. Fill me with courage and resilience. Remind me of your presence and protection in moments of weakness or danger. Guide me in righteousness and give me discernment to avoid harmful situations. Strengthen my faith and trust in you as my ultimate protector. Thank you for being my strength and shield. May I always find refuge and security in you. May your name be glorified in my life.

In Jesus' name, I pray.

Amen.

Day 6: "I affirm that God is my comforter. He comforts me in all my troubles, and His peace surpasses all understanding." (2 Corinthians 1:3-4)

Prayer

Heavenly Father,

You are my comforter. I surrender my troubles and burdens to you. Please surround me with your comforting presence and bring solace to my heart. Help me find rest in your loving arms and trust in your perfect plan.

Remind me of your presence in moments of distress or sorrow. Fill me with your peace that surpasses understanding. Give me strength and courage, knowing you are by my side. Thank you for being my comforter. May your presence bring strength and hope. May your peace guide me.

In Jesus' name, I pray.

Amen.

Day 7: "I affirm that God is my rock and my fortress. He is my stronghold in times of trouble, and I find refuge in Him." (Psalm 18:2)

Prayer

Heavenly Father,

You are my rock and fortress. I surrender my fears and anxieties to you. Guide me through challenges and give me strength and courage. Remind me of your presence in times of trouble. Be my refuge and shield me from harm. Provide me with the strength to overcome obstacles. Thank you for being my rock and fortress. May I always find refuge and security in you. May your presence bring peace and protection. May your name be glorified in my life.

In Jesus' name, I pray.

Amen.

Day 8: "I affirm that God is my guide. He leads me on the path of righteousness and directs my steps in the way I should go." (Psalm 32:8)

Prayer

Heavenly Father,

You are my guide. I surrender my plans and desires to you. Please guide and direct me in all my decisions. Help me align my will with yours and follow the path you have set before me. Give me the discernment to recognize your voice and the courage to obey your leading. Remind me of your guiding presence in moments of confusion or uncertainty. Illuminate my path and show me the way I should go. Thank you for being my guide. May I always seek your will and follow your leading. May your guidance bring clarity and purpose to my life. May your name be glorified in all that I do.

In Jesus' name, I pray.

Amen.

Day 9: "I affirm that God is my restorer. He restores my soul and brings beauty from ashes." (Psalm 23:3)

Prayer

Heavenly Father,

You are my restorer. I surrender my brokenness and pain to you. Please heal my weary soul and bring comfort to my heart. Help me let go of the past and embrace new beginnings. Remind me of your restoring presence in moments of despair. Renew my strength and fill me with your peace. Show me the beauty that can arise from the ashes of my life. Give me the courage to trust in your restoration process. Thank you for being my restorer. May your touch bring beauty, and may your restoration bring glory to your name.

In Jesus' name, I pray.

Amen.

Day 10: "I affirm that God is my peace. He gives me peace that surpasses all understanding, even in the midst of betrayal and disappointment." (Philippians 4:7)

Prayer

Heavenly Father,

You are my peace. I surrender my hurts and disappointments to you. Please bring healing and peace to my wounded soul. Help me forgive and release any bitterness or resentment. Fill me with your peace that transcends all circumstances. Remind me of your peace in moments of betrayal or disappointment. Calm the storms within me and bring tranquility to my soul. Help me find solace in your presence and trust in your plan. Thank you for being my peace. May your peace guard my heart and mind. May your peace shine through me, even in difficult circumstances.

May your name be glorified.

In Jesus' name, I pray.

Amen.

Day 11: "I affirm that God is my defender. He fights for me and vindicates me in the face of betrayal and disappointment." (Psalm 34:22)

Prayer

Heavenly Father,

You are my defender. I surrender the pain of betrayal and disappointment to you. Give me strength and courage to rise above these circumstances. Help me forgive and release any bitterness. Fill me with your peace and assurance. Remind me of your presence and promise to fight for me. Shield me and bring justice. Help me trust in your timing and have patience. Thank you for being my defender. May your presence bring comfort and strength. May your name be glorified.

In Jesus' name, I pray.

Amen.

Day 12: "I affirm that God is my refuge and strength, a very present help in times of trouble. I find comfort and strength in His presence, knowing that He will never leave me nor forsake me." (Psalm 46:1

Prayer

Heavenly Father,

You are my refuge and strength. I surrender my troubles and burdens to you. Please be my refuge and give me strength in difficult times. Help me find solace in your loving arms and trust in your unfailing love. Remind me of your presence in moments of trouble or distress. Be my safe haven, and give me the courage to face each day. Thank you for being my refuge and strength. I trust in your promise to never leave me. May your presence bring comfort and peace. May your name be glorified.

In Jesus' name, I pray.

Amen.

Day 13: "I affirm that God is faithful, even when others may betray or disappoint me. I trust in His unfailing love and His plans for my life." (Psalm 36:5)

Prayer

Heavenly Father,

You are faithful. I surrender my hurts and disappointments to you. Please heal my broken heart and help me forgive. Fill me with your love and peace. Remind me of your faithfulness in moments of betrayal or disappointment. Help me trust in your timing and have patience. Give me the strength and courage to keep moving forward. Thank you for your faithfulness. I trust in your love and plans for my life. May your faithfulness bring healing and restoration. May your name be glorified.

In Jesus' name, I pray.

Amen.

Day 14: "I affirm that God is my healer. He binds up the brokenhearted and brings restoration and healing to my wounded soul." (Psalm 147:3)

Prayer

Heavenly Father,

You are my healer. I surrender my brokenness and pain to you. Please mend my wounded soul and bring restoration to my heart and mind. Help me release bitterness and forgive those who have hurt me. Remind me of your healing presence in moments of despair. Pour out your love and grace, bringing comfort and peace. I trust in your perfect timing and have patience as I wait for healing. Thank you for being my healer. May your touch bring wholeness and peace to my life. May your name be glorified.

In Jesus' name, I pray.

Amen.

Day 15: "I affirm that God is my provider. He meets all my needs according to His riches in glory, and He will never leave me lacking." (Philippians 4:19)

Prayer

Heavenly Father,

You are my provider. I surrender my worries and anxieties about provision to you. Please provide for my financial and material needs. Help me trust in your abundance and be a good steward of what you have given me. Remind me of your provision in moments of lack or uncertainty. Open doors of opportunity

and bless the work of my hands. Give me the wisdom to make wise financial decisions. Thank you for being my provider. May your provision bring peace and security. May your name be glorified.

In Jesus' name, I pray.

Amen.

Day 16: "I affirm that God is my strength and my shield. He gives me the strength to persevere through difficult times and protects me from harm." (Psalm 28:7)

Prayer

Heavenly Father,

You are my strength and shield. I surrender my weaknesses and vulnerabilities to you. Please give me the strength to face challenges and trials. Help me rely on your power and fill me with courage and perseverance. Remind me of your strength and protection in moments of weakness or danger. Be my shield and guide me on the right path. Thank you for being my strength and shield. May your name be glorified.

In Jesus' name, I pray.

Amen.

Day 17: "I affirm that God is my comforter. He comforts me in all my troubles, and His peace surpasses all understanding." (2 Corinthians 1:3-4)

Prayer

Heavenly Father,

You are my comforter. I surrender my troubles and burdens to you. Please surround me with your comforting presence and bring peace to my troubled heart. Help me find rest in your loving arms and trust in your unfailing love. Remind me of your comforting presence in moments of distress or sorrow. Pour out your peace and calm the storms within me. Thank you for being my comforter. May your presence bring healing and restoration. May your name be glorified.

In Jesus' name, I pray.

Amen.

Day 18: "I affirm that God is my rock and my fortress. He is my stronghold in times of trouble, and I find refuge in Him." (Psalm 18:2)

Prayer

Father, in the name of Jesus, thank you for being my rock and fortress. I surrender my fears and anxieties to you. Please give me the strength to face adversity and help me rely on you as my unshakable rock. Be my fortress, guarding me and providing a safe haven in life's storms.

Remind me of your steadfastness in times of trouble. Help me find refuge in you, knowing you are my ever-present help. Give me the courage to trust in your unfailing love and promises.

Thank you for being my rock and fortress. I trust in your faithfulness to protect and strengthen me. May your presence bring peace and security. May your name be glorified.

In Jesus' name, I pray.

Amen.

Day 19: "I affirm that God is my guide. He leads me on the path of righteousness and directs my steps in the way I should go." (Psalm 32:8)

Prayer

Heavenly Father,

You are my guide. I surrender my plans and desires to you. Please guide me and give me wisdom in all areas of my life. Help me trust in your leading and follow your voice. Open my ears to hear your whispers and my heart to discern your will.

Remind me of your presence in moments of confusion or uncertainty. Illuminate my path and give me clarity in my decisions. Help me walk in obedience to your Word and trust in your perfect plan.

Thank you for being my guide. I trust in your faithfulness to lead me on the right path. May your guidance bring peace and fulfillment. May your name be glorified.

In Jesus' name, I pray.

Amen.

Day 20: "I affirm that God is my restorer. He restores my soul and brings beauty from ashes." (Psalm 23:3)

Prayer

Heavenly Father,

You are my restorer. I surrender my brokenness and pain to you. Please heal my wounded soul and bring beauty from the ashes of my past. Turn my mourning into joy, and help me trust in your redeeming power. Remind me of your restoring presence in moments of despair. Pour out your love and grace, bringing comfort and peace. Thank you for being my restorer. May your name be glorified.

In Jesus' name, I pray.

Amen.

Day 21: "I affirm that God is my peace. He gives me peace that surpasses all understanding, even in the midst of betrayal and disappointment." (Philippians 4:7)

Prayer

Heavenly Father,

You are my peace. I surrender my hurts and disappointments to you. Please fill me with your peace and guard my heart and mind. Help me release bitterness and forgive those who have hurt me. Give me strength to let go of pain and walk in your peace.

Remind me of your peace in moments of turmoil. Quiet the storms within me and bring serenity to my soul. Help me trust in your sovereignty and have faith that you are working all things for my good.

Thank you for being my peace. I trust in your faithfulness to bring calm in difficult times.

May your peace guard me. May your name be glorified.

In Jesus' name, I pray.

Amen.

Day 22: "I affirm that God is my defender. He fights for me and vindicates me in the face of betrayal and disappointment." (Psalm 34:22)

Prayer

Heavenly Father,

You are my defender. I surrender my hurts and feelings of betrayal to you. Please defend and protect me in these challenges. Help me trust in your justice and find solace in your presence. Strengthen me to forgive and walk in love and grace.

Remind me of your defending presence in moments of injustice or disappointment. Shield me and bring justice to my situation. Help me lean on you and find comfort in your unfailing love.

Thank you for being my defender. I trust in your faithfulness to fight for me and bring vindication. May your defense bring healing and restoration. May your name be glorified.

In Jesus' name, I pray.

Amen.

Day 23: "I affirm that God is my refuge and strength, a very present help in times of trouble. I find comfort and strength in His presence, knowing that He will never leave me nor forsake me." (Psalm 46:1)

Prayer

Heavenly Father,

You are my refuge and strength, always present in times of trouble. I surrender my burdens to you and ask for your strength and protection. Help me find solace in your presence and trust in your unfailing love. Be my safe haven, and give me peace that surpasses understanding. Thank you for being my refuge and strength. May your name be glorified.

In Jesus' name, I pray.

Amen.

Day 24: "I affirm that God is faithful, even when others may betray or disappoint me. I trust in His unfailing love and His plans for my life." (Psalm 36:5)

Prayer

Heavenly Father,

You are faithful. I surrender my hurts and disappointments to you. Please heal and comfort me. Help me forgive those who have hurt me and let go of bitterness. Remind me of your faithfulness in times of pain and confusion. Guide me on the path of righteousness and lead me to the abundant life you have for me.

Thank you for your faithfulness. I trust in your love and plans for my life. May your faithfulness bring healing and restoration. May your name be glorified.

In Jesus' name, I pray.

Amen.

Day 25: "I affirm that God is my healer. He binds up the brokenhearted and brings restoration and healing to my wounded soul." (Psalm 147:3)

Prayer

Heavenly Father,

You are my healer. I surrender my brokenness and pain to you. Please heal my wounded soul and bring restoration to every area of my life. Help me trust in your redeeming power and have faith in your ability to make all things new.

Remind me of your healing presence in moments of despair. Pour out your love and grace, bringing comfort and peace. I surrender my burdens to you and find rest in your healing embrace.

Thank you for being my healer. I trust in your faithfulness to bring restoration and healing.

May your touch bring wholeness and peace to my life. May your name be glorified.

In Jesus' name, I pray.

Amen.

Day 26: "I affirm that God is my provider. He meets all my needs according to His riches in glory, and He will never leave me lacking." (Philippians 4:19)

Prayer

Heavenly Father,

You are my provider. I surrender my worries and anxieties about provision to you. Please provide for me and guide me in every area of my life. Help me trust in your abundance and have faith that you will meet all my needs. Give me wisdom to steward the resources you have given me.

Remind me of your provision in moments of uncertainty or lack. Open doors of opportunity and bless the work of my hands. Help me be a good steward and use my blessings to bless others.

Thank you for being my provider. I trust in your faithfulness. May your provision bring abundance and blessings to my life. May your name be glorified.

In Jesus' name, I pray.

Amen.

Day 27: "I affirm that God is my strength and my shield. He gives me the strength to persevere through difficult times and protects me from harm." (Psalm 28:7)

Prayer

Heavenly Father,

You are my strength and shield. I surrender my weaknesses to you and ask for your strength to sustain me. Help me rely on your power and face challenges with confidence. Remind me of your strength in moments of weakness and fear. Empower me to overcome obstacles and guide me on the path of righteousness. Thank you for being my strength and shield. May your name be glorified.

In Jesus' name, I pray.

Amen.

Day 28: "I affirm that God is my comforter. He comforts me in all my troubles, and His peace surpasses all understanding." (2 Corinthians 1:3-4)

Prayer

Heavenly Father,

You are my comforter. I surrender my troubles and burdens to you. Please surround me with your comforting presence and help me find rest in your embrace. Give me the strength to lean on you and find peace in your unfailing love. Remind me of your comforting touch in moments of distress or sorrow. Pour out your peace upon me and calm the storms within me. Thank you for being my comforter. I trust in your faithfulness to bring comfort and peace in all my troubles. May your comfort bring healing and restoration. May your name be glorified.

In Jesus' name, I pray.

Amen.

Day 29: "I affirm that God is my rock and my fortress. He is my stronghold in times of trouble, and I find refuge in Him." (Psalm 18:2)

Prayer

Heavenly Father,

You are my rock and fortress. I surrender my fears and anxieties to you. Please give me strength and protection in the midst of challenges. Help me find shelter in your presence and trust in your unfailing love. Remind me of your steadfastness in moments of uncertainty or danger. Be my rock, providing stability and security. Thank you for being my stronghold. May your presence bring peace and security to my life. May your name be glorified.

In Jesus' name, I pray.

Amen.

FORGIVENESS

Day 1: "I affirm that I choose to forgive those who have wronged me, just as Christ has forgiven me. I release any bitterness and resentment, and I choose to walk in love and forgiveness." (Ephesians 4:32)

Prayer

Heavenly Father,

I choose to forgive those who have wronged me, just as Christ has forgiven me. I release any bitterness and resentment from my heart and surrender these hurts to you. Please heal me and help me walk in love and forgiveness.

Give me the grace to extend mercy and compassion to others, as you have shown me. Strengthen me to let go of grudges and negative feelings and to embrace a heart of forgiveness.

Remind me of your forgiveness in moments of pain or hurt. Help me see others through your eyes and extend grace and understanding. Fill me with your love so I can be a vessel of reconciliation and healing.

Thank you, Lord, for your forgiveness and grace. I choose to forgive as you have forgiven me. May your love and forgiveness flow through me, bringing healing and restoration. May your name be glorified.

In Jesus' name, I pray.

Amen.

Day 2: "I declare that I will not hold onto grudges or seek revenge. I trust in God's justice and His ability to bring healing and restoration." (Romans 12:19)

Prayer

Heavenly Father,

I surrender my desire for revenge to you. Help me release any bitterness or anger I may be holding onto. Fill my heart with your love and forgiveness so I can extend grace to those who have wronged me. Remind me of your sovereignty in moments of hurt or injustice. Give me the strength to forgive and let go of any desire for revenge. Thank you for your justice and ability to bring healing and restoration. May your love and forgiveness flow through me, bringing reconciliation and peace.

May your name be glorified.

In Jesus' name, I pray.

Amen.

Day 3: "I affirm that forgiveness is a choice, not a feeling. I choose to forgive, even when it is difficult, knowing that God's grace is sufficient for me." (2 Corinthians 12:9)

Prayer

Heavenly Father,

I choose to forgive, even when it is difficult, knowing that your grace is sufficient for me. Fill my heart with your grace and help me extend forgiveness to those who have hurt me. Give me the strength to let go of grudges and embrace a heart of forgiveness. Remind me of your unfailing love and mercy in moments when forgiveness feels impossible. Help me see others through your eyes and extend grace and understanding. Fill me with your Holy Spirit so I may walk in forgiveness and be a vessel of reconciliation. Thank you for your grace and sufficiency. May your forgiveness flow through me, bringing healing and restoration. May your name be glorified.

In Jesus' name, I pray.

Amen.

Day 4: "I declare that I will not allow the actions of others to define me. I am a child of God, and my identity is found in Him alone." (1 John 3:1)

Prayer

Heavenly Father,

I declare that I will not let others define me. My identity is found in you alone as a child of God. Remind me that my worth and value come from you. Fill me with your truth and assurance so I can confidently walk into who you created me to be. Help me find my worth in your love and acceptance, not in seeking validation from others. Thank you for reminding me of my true identity. I am a child of God, and that is enough. May I live each day with confidence and purpose, knowing I am loved and cherished by you. May your name be glorified.

In Jesus' name, I pray.

Amen.

Day 5: "I affirm that forgiveness is a process, and I will give myself grace as I work through my emotions. I will lean on God's strength to help me forgive." (Philippians 4:13)

Prayer

Heavenly Father,

I acknowledge that forgiveness is a process. Please guide me through this journey and give me the grace and strength I need. I surrender my pain and hurt to you, asking for help in releasing any bitterness or anger. Fill me with your love and compassion so I can extend grace to those who have hurt me. Remind me of your power and strength when forgiveness feels impossible. Help me trust in your ability to help me forgive and give me the courage to let go of past hurts. Thank you for your grace and strength. I know that I can do all things through Christ who strengthens me. May your strength empower me to forgive and find healing. May your name be glorified.

In Jesus' name, I pray.

Amen.

Day 6: "I declare that I will not dwell on past hurts or allow bitterness to take root in my heart. I will focus on the future and the freedom that comes from forgiveness." (Philippians 3:13-14)

Prayer

Heavenly Father,

I choose to let go of past hurts and focus on the future. I surrender any pain or bitterness to you and ask for your healing touch. Fill me with your love and grace so I can walk in forgiveness and experience freedom. Remind me of your faithfulness and the new beginnings you offer. Help me to press on toward the goal, knowing you are with me. Thank you for the freedom that comes from forgiveness. May your love and grace guide me. May your name be glorified.

In Jesus' name, I pray.

Amen.

Day 7: "I affirm that forgiveness is a gift I give myself. By forgiving others, I release the burden of carrying resentment and open myself up to God's healing." (Matthew 6:14-15)

Prayer

Heavenly Father,

I choose to release the burden of resentment and open myself up to your healing. Help me let go of grudges and replace them with your love and grace. Fill me with your Holy Spirit so I may walk in forgiveness and experience freedom. Remind me of your love and mercy when pain resurfaces. Give me the strength to release negative feelings and embrace forgiveness. Thank you for the gift of forgiveness. May your love and grace flow through me, bringing reconciliation and peace. May your name be glorified.

In Jesus' name, I pray.

Amen.

Day 8: "I declare that I will not allow unforgiveness to hinder my relationship with God. I will seek His guidance and strength as I navigate the process of forgiveness." (Psalm 32:5)

Prayer

Heavenly Father,

I surrender any unforgiveness in my heart to you. Please heal my brokenness and help me release grudges with your love and grace. Fill me with your Holy Spirit so I can walk in forgiveness and experience freedom. Guide me in seeking reconciliation and give me the wisdom to know when to extend forgiveness and set boundaries. I rely on your strength and promise to never leave me. Thank you for your guidance and strength. May your love and grace bring healing and restoration. Strengthen my relationship with you as I choose to forgive. May your name be glorified.

In Jesus' name, I pray.

Amen.

Day 9: "I affirm that forgiveness does not excuse the actions of others, but it frees me from the power they hold over me. I choose to walk in freedom and peace." (Colossians 3:13)

Prayer

Heavenly Father,

I surrender any resentment or bitterness in my heart to you. Please heal the wounds caused by others and help me release their power over me. Fill me with your love and grace so I can walk in forgiveness and experience freedom. Remind me of your love and mercy when pain resurfaces. Give me the strength to release negative feelings and embrace forgiveness. Thank you for the freedom and peace that come from forgiveness. May your love and grace bring reconciliation and peace. May your name be glorified.

In Jesus' name, I pray.

Amen.

Day 10: "I declare that I will not allow bitterness to poison my heart. I will guard my heart and fill it with love, compassion, and forgiveness." (Proverbs 4:23)

Prayer

Heavenly Father,

I surrender any bitterness or resentment in my heart to you. Please cleanse and purify my heart, replacing negative emotions with your love and compassion. Fill me with your Holy Spirit so I can walk in forgiveness and extend grace to those who have hurt me. Remind me of your unfailing love and the example of forgiveness you have shown me. Help me see others through your eyes and respond with kindness and understanding. Give me the strength to release grudges and embrace a heart of forgiveness. Thank you for your grace and mercy. May your love flow through me, bringing healing and reconciliation. May your name be glorified.

In Jesus' name, I pray.

Amen.

Day 11: "I affirm that forgiveness is an act of obedience to God. I will follow His example and forgive others, just as He has forgiven me." (Ephesians 5:1-2)

Prayer

Heavenly Father,

I choose to forgive others as you have forgiven me. Fill me with your love and compassion so I can let go of grudges and resentment. Help me see others through your eyes and respond with grace and mercy. Give me the courage to release bitterness and embrace forgiveness. Thank you for the power of forgiveness to bring healing and restoration. May your love and grace flow through me, bringing reconciliation and peace. May your name be glorified.

In Jesus' name, I pray.

Amen.

Day 12: "I declare that forgiveness is a reflection of God's love and mercy. I will extend grace to those who have wronged me, knowing that I too have received God's grace." (Luke 6:36)

Prayer

Heavenly Father,

I choose to extend grace and forgiveness to those who have wronged me. Fill me with your love and compassion so I can let go of grudges and resentment. Help me see others through your eyes and respond with mercy and compassion. Give me the courage to release bitterness and embrace forgiveness. Thank you for your unfailing love and grace. May your love and grace flow through me, bringing reconciliation and peace. May your name be glorified.

In Jesus' name, I pray.

Amen.

Day 13: "I affirm that forgiveness is a choice to let go of the past and embrace a future filled with hope and healing. I will trust in God's plan for my life." (Jeremiah 29:11)

Prayer

Heavenly Father,

I choose to let go of the past and embrace a future filled with hope and healing. I surrender any pain or hurt to you and release any grudges or resentment. Fill me with your love and grace so I can walk in forgiveness and experience the hope and healing that come from letting go. Remind me of your faithfulness and the plans you have for me. Help me trust in your timing and purpose for my life. Give me the strength to let go and press forward toward the future you have prepared for me. Thank you for your guidance and provision. May your love and grace bring restoration and joy. May your name be glorified.

In Jesus' name, I pray.

Amen.

Day 14: "I declare that forgiveness is a process of surrendering my pain and hurt to God. I will allow Him to heal my wounds and restore my heart." (Psalm 147:3)

Prayer

Heavenly Father,

I surrender my pain and hurt to you, trusting in your healing power and ability to restore my heart. Help me release bitterness and replace it with your love and grace. Fill me with your Holy Spirit so I can walk in forgiveness and experience healing. Remind me of your faithfulness, and give me strength to surrender my pain to you. Thank you for your love and compassion.

May your healing touch bring wholeness to my heart, and may your name be glorified.

In Jesus' name, I pray.

Amen.

Day 15: "I affirm that forgiveness is an act of faith. I will trust in God's ability to bring beauty from ashes and turn my pain into something purposeful." (Romans 8:28)

Prayer

Heavenly Father,

I trust in your ability to bring beauty from ashes and turn my pain into something purposeful. I surrender my pain and hurt to you, knowing that you are able to bring good out of every situation. Help me have faith in your ability to redeem and restore. Remind me of your faithfulness and the power of your love. Give me the strength to let go of the past and embrace the purpose you have for me. Thank you for your promise to bring beauty from ashes. May your name be glorified.

In Jesus' name, I pray.

Amen.

Day 16: "I declare that forgiveness is a choice to break free from the cycle of hurt and bitterness. I will choose to forgive, even if the other person does not apologize or change." (Matthew 18:21-22)

Prayer

Heavenly Father,

I choose to break free from the cycle of hurt and bitterness through forgiveness. I surrender my feelings of hurt and bitterness to you and ask for your strength and grace to release any grudges. Fill me with your love and compassion so I can experience the freedom that comes from forgiveness. Remind me of your love and forgiveness towards me, and help me see others through your eyes. Give me the courage to let go of resentment and embrace a heart of forgiveness. Thank you for the power of forgiveness to bring healing and restoration. May your love and grace flow through me, bringing reconciliation and peace. May your name be glorified.

In Jesus' name, I pray.

Amen.

Day 17: "I affirm that forgiveness is a daily decision. I will choose to forgive, even when memories resurface or emotions arise. I will rely on God's strength to help me." (Luke 17:4)

Prayer

Heavenly Father,

I choose to forgive daily, even when memories resurface or emotions arise. I rely on your strength to help me. Fill me with your love and compassion so I can extend forgiveness to those who have hurt me. Remind me of your faithfulness and ability to heal. Help me trust in your guidance and give me the courage to choose forgiveness. Thank you for your unfailing love and the power of forgiveness. May your love and compassion flow through me, bringing reconciliation and peace. May your name be glorified.

In Jesus' name, I pray.

Amen.

Day 18: "I declare that forgiveness is an act of humility. I will humble myself before God and others, recognizing that I too am in need of forgiveness." (Colossians 3:12-13)

Prayer

Heavenly Father,

I acknowledge that forgiveness is an act of humility. I surrender my pride to you and ask for your help in seeing myself through your eyes. Fill me with your humility and grace so I can extend forgiveness to others with a humble heart. Remind me of your love and mercy towards me, and give me the strength to lay down my pride. Thank you for your forgiveness and grace. May your humility and grace flow through me, bringing reconciliation and peace. May your name be glorified.

In Jesus' name, I pray.

Amen.

Day 19: "I affirm that forgiveness is a process of healing and restoration. I will allow God to work in my heart and bring healing to the broken places." (Psalm 147:3)

Prayer

Heavenly Father,

I surrender myself to you, knowing that forgiveness is a process of healing and restoration. I ask for your healing touch to mend the brokenness within me. Fill me with your love and compassion so I can extend forgiveness to those who have wronged me. Remind me of your promise to heal the brokenhearted and bind up their wounds. Help me trust in your process and timing. Give me the strength to continue on this journey of forgiveness, knowing you are with me every step of the way. Thank you for your faithfulness and desire to bring healing and restoration. May your name be glorified.

In Jesus' name, I pray.

Amen.

Day 20: "I declare that forgiveness is a choice to break the chains of bitterness and resentment. I will choose to walk in freedom and extend forgiveness to others." (Galatians 5:1)

Prayer

Heavenly Father,

I choose to break free from bitterness and resentment through forgiveness. I surrender these feelings to you and ask for your strength and grace to help me. Fill me with your love and compassion so I can extend forgiveness to those who have wronged me. Remind me of your love and mercy towards me, and help me see others through your eyes. Give me the courage to let go of the past and embrace a heart of forgiveness. Thank you for the freedom that comes from choosing forgiveness. May your love and grace flow through me, bringing reconciliation and peace. May your name be glorified.

In Jesus' name, I pray.

Amen.

Day 21: "I affirm that forgiveness is an act of love. I will choose to love my enemies and pray for those who have wronged me, knowing that love has the power to transform hearts." (Matthew 5:44)

Prayer

Heavenly Father,

I choose to love my enemies and pray for those who have wronged me. Fill my heart with your love and grace so I can extend forgiveness and love to them. Help me see them through your eyes and respond with compassion and kindness. Remind me of your great love for me and give me the strength to lay down my pride. Thank you for your unconditional love and the power of forgiveness. May your love and grace flow through me, bringing reconciliation and peace. May your name be glorified.

In Jesus' name, I pray.

Amen.

Day 22: "I declare that forgiveness is a journey of growth and maturity. I will allow God to shape my character and teach me to love and forgive as He does." (Ephesians 4:32)

Prayer

Heavenly Father,

I surrender myself to you, asking for your guidance in the journey of forgiveness. Help me let go of pride, bitterness, and resentment. Fill me with your love and compassion so I may reflect your character. Remind me of your grace and mercy, and give me the courage to face unforgiveness in my heart. Thank you for shaping my character and teaching me to love and forgive. May your love and grace flow through me, bringing growth and maturity. May your name be glorified.

In Jesus' name, I pray.

Amen.

Day 23: "I affirm that forgiveness is a choice to let go of the past and embrace a future filled with hope and healing. I will trust in God's plan for my life." (Jeremiah 29:11)

Prayer

Heavenly Father,

I choose to let go of the past and embrace a future filled with hope and healing. I trust in your plan for my life, knowing that you are faithful and will work all things together for my good. I surrender any pain or hurt from the past to you, asking for your healing touch to restore my heart. Fill me with your hope and peace so I can move forward with confidence. Thank you for your love and grace. May your hope and peace guide me as I trust in your plan. May your name be glorified.

In Jesus' name, I pray.

Amen.

Day 24: "I declare that forgiveness is an act of surrender. I will surrender my pain, anger, and resentment to God, allowing Him to heal and restore my heart." (Psalm 34:18)

Prayer

Heavenly Father,

I surrender my pain, anger, and resentment to you. I ask for your healing touch to bring restoration and wholeness to my heart. Remind me of your promise to be near to the brokenhearted. Help me trust in your presence and your ability to bring healing and restoration. Fill me with your love and compassion so I can extend forgiveness to those who have wronged me. Thank you for your faithfulness and desire to heal and restore. May your name be glorified.

In Jesus' name, I pray.

Amen.

Day 25: "I affirm that forgiveness is a choice to break free from the chains of bitterness and resentment. I will choose to forgive, knowing that it is for my own freedom and peace." (Colossians 3:13)

Prayer

Heavenly Father,

I choose to break free from bitterness and resentment through forgiveness. I surrender these feelings to you and ask for your strength and grace to help me. Fill me with your love and compassion so I can extend forgiveness to those who have wronged me. Remind me of your love and mercy towards me, and help me see others through your eyes. Give me the courage to let go of the past and embrace a heart of forgiveness. Thank you for the freedom that comes from choosing forgiveness. May your love and grace flow through me, bringing reconciliation and peace. May your name be glorified.

In Jesus' name, I pray.

Amen.

Day 26: "I declare that forgiveness is an act of obedience to God. I will follow His example and forgive others, just as He has forgiven me." (Ephesians 4:32)

Prayer

Heavenly Father,

I choose to forgive others as you have forgiven me. Fill me with your love and compassion so I may extend forgiveness to those who have wronged me. Remind me of your great love and mercy, and give me the courage to let go of hurt and pain. Thank you for empowering me to forgive. May your love and grace flow through me, bringing reconciliation and peace. May your name be glorified.

In Jesus' name, I pray.

Amen.

Day 27: "I affirm that forgiveness is a process of healing and restoration. I will allow God to work in my heart and bring healing to the broken places." (Psalm 147:3)

Prayer

Heavenly Father,

I surrender myself to you, asking for your healing touch to bring restoration and wholeness to my heart. Help me release any bitterness or resentment that hinders the healing process. Fill me with your love and compassion so I may extend forgiveness to those who have wronged me. Remind me of your faithfulness and give me the strength to persevere on the path of healing and forgiveness. Thank you for your love and grace. May your name be glorified.

In Jesus' name, I pray.

Amen.

Day 28: "I declare that forgiveness is a choice to break the cycle of hurt and bitterness. I will choose to forgive, even if the other person does not apologize or change." (Matthew 18:21-22)

Prayer

Heavenly Father,

I choose to break the cycle of hurt and bitterness through forgiveness. I surrender my feelings of hurt and bitterness to you. Fill me with your love and compassion so I can extend forgiveness to those who have wronged me, regardless of their response. Remind me of your great love and mercy towards me. Help me to break the cycle of hurt and bitterness and to extend forgiveness as an act of obedience to you. Thank you for empowering me to break this cycle through forgiveness. May your love and grace bring healing and restoration. May your name be glorified.

In Jesus' name, I pray.

Amen.

Day 29: "I affirm that forgiveness is an act of humility. I will humble myself before God and others, recognizing that I too am in need of forgiveness." (Colossians 3:12-13)

Prayer

Heavenly Father,

I humbly come before you, recognizing that forgiveness is an act of humility. I surrender any pride or self-righteousness that hinders my ability to forgive. Fill me with your love and compassion so I may extend forgiveness to those who have wronged me. Remind me of your great love and mercy, and help me admit my own faults. Thank you for your forgiveness and grace. May your love and grace flow through me, bringing reconciliation and peace.

May your name be glorified.

In Jesus' name, I pray.

Amen.

Day 30: "I declare that forgiveness is a journey of growth and maturity. I will allow God to shape my character and teach me to love and forgive as He does." (Ephesians 4:32)

Prayer

Heavenly Father,

I surrender myself to you, asking for your guidance and strength on the journey of forgiveness. Help me grow in maturity and develop a heart that is quick to forgive. Fill me with your love and compassion so I may extend forgiveness to those who have wronged me. Teach me to let go of grudges and see others through your eyes. Remind me of your love and mercy when forgiveness feels challenging. Thank you for your guidance and grace. May your love and grace flow through me, bringing reconciliation and peace. May your name be glorified.

In Jesus' name, I pray.

Amen.

Day 31: "I affirm that forgiveness is a choice to let go of the past and embrace a future filled with hope and healing. I will trust in God's plan for my life." (Jeremiah 29:11)

Prayer

Heavenly Father,

I choose to let go of the past and embrace a future filled with hope and healing. I surrender my pain, hurt, and disappointment to you. Please heal my heart and help me release any bitterness or resentment. Fill me with your love and compassion so I can extend forgiveness to those who have wronged me. Remind me of your promise of hope and healing, and give me the strength to trust in your plan for my life. Thank you for your love and grace. May your name be glorified.

In Jesus' name, I pray.

Amen.

May these affirmations and declarations guide you on your journey of forgiveness. Remember that forgiveness is a process, and God is with you every step of the way. Trust in His grace and allow His love to heal your heart.

Amen.

HEALING HEART

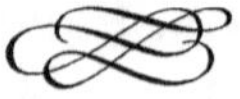

Day 1: "I affirm that God is the ultimate healer of hearts. I declare that His love and grace are more than enough to heal any pain or brokenness within me." (Psalm 147:3)

Prayer

Heavenly Father,

You are the ultimate healer of hearts. Your love and grace are more than enough to heal any pain or brokenness within me. I surrender my pain and brokenness to you. Pour out your love and grace upon me, bringing restoration and wholeness. I trust in your power to heal and believe that you are able to mend what is broken.

Remind me of your love and faithfulness in moments of overwhelming pain. Help me find comfort in your presence and fill me with your peace. Thank you for your healing touch. May your love and grace flow through me, bringing restoration and wholeness. May your name be glorified.

In Jesus' name, I pray.

Amen.

Day 2: "I affirm that God's healing power is at work in my heart. I declare that He is restoring and renewing me from the inside out." (Isaiah 61:1)

Prayer

Heavenly Father,

I affirm that your healing power is at work in my heart. I surrender myself to your touch, inviting you to restore and renew me from the inside out. Pour out your love and grace, washing away any pain or brokenness. I trust in your power to heal and make all things new.

Remind me of your faithfulness in moments of doubt or discouragement. Help me hold onto the truth that you are working in my heart, even when I can't see it. Fill me with hope and confidence in your healing process.

Thank you for your healing power. Continue to restore and renew me, bringing wholeness and transformation. May your name be glorified.

In Jesus' name, I pray.

Amen.

Day 3: "I affirm that God's healing is not limited by time or circumstance. I declare that He is able to heal even the deepest wounds and bring beauty from ashes." (Jeremiah 30:17)

Prayer

Heavenly Father,

I affirm that your healing power is not limited by time or circumstance. You are able to heal even the deepest wounds and bring beauty from ashes. I surrender my wounds and hurts to you, inviting you to bring healing and restoration. Pour out your love and grace upon me, transforming my pain into something beautiful. Remind me of your faithfulness in moments of doubt or despair. Help me hold onto the truth that you are able to heal and restore, no matter how long it takes or how difficult the circumstances may be. Fill me with hope and confidence in your healing power. Thank you for your unlimited healing. May your name be glorified as your healing power flows through me, bringing restoration and transformation.

In Jesus' name, I pray.

Amen.

Day 4: "I affirm that God's healing is a process. I declare that I will trust in His timing and allow Him to work in me, knowing that He is faithful to complete the good work He has started." (Philippians 1:6)

Prayer

Heavenly Father,

I trust in your timing and surrender myself to your healing process. Fill me with patience and perseverance, knowing that you are at work in every season of my life. Remind me of your faithfulness when doubt or impatience arises. Help me to trust in your perfect plan and surrender control. Thank you for your healing process. May your name be glorified as your healing power brings restoration and wholeness.

In Jesus' name, I pray.

Amen.

Day 5: "I affirm that God's healing is not just physical, but emotional and spiritual as well. I declare that He is healing every part of me, bringing wholeness and restoration." (Psalm 34:18)

Prayer

Heavenly Father,

I affirm today that your healing extends to every part of my being. I surrender myself to your touch, inviting you to heal my heart and soul. Pour out your love and grace, bringing restoration to every area of my life. Remind me of your faithfulness in moments of discouragement. Fill me with hope and confidence in your healing power. Thank you for your touch. I declare that you are healing me, bringing wholeness and restoration. May your name be glorified.

In Jesus' name, I pray.

Amen.

Day 6: "I affirm that God's healing is available to all who seek Him. I declare that as I draw near to Him, He will draw near to me and bring healing to my heart." (James 4:8)

Prayer

Heavenly Father,

I affirm today that your healing is available to all who seek you. As I draw near to you, I trust that you will draw near to me and bring healing to my heart. Pour out your love and grace upon me, restoring and renewing me. Remind me of your faithfulness in moments of doubt or fear. Fill me with hope and confidence in your healing power. Thank you for your willingness to heal. May your name be glorified as your healing power flows through me, bringing restoration and wholeness.

In Jesus' name, I pray.

Amen.

Day 7: "I affirm that God's healing is a result of His great love for me. I declare that His love is powerful enough to heal any hurt or pain I may be experiencing." (1 John 4:9)

Prayer

Heavenly Father,

I affirm today that your love is powerful enough to heal any hurt or pain I may be experiencing. I surrender my hurts and pains to you, inviting you to pour out your love upon me and bring healing and restoration. Remind me of your faithfulness when fear or doubt arises. Fill me with confidence in your healing power. Thank you for your great love and healing. May your love continue to flow through me, bringing healing and restoration. May your name be glorified.

In Jesus' name, I pray.

Amen.

Day 8: "I affirm that God's healing is not dependent on my own strength or efforts. I declare that His healing power is made perfect in my weakness, and I will rely on Him for healing." (2 Corinthians 12:9)

Prayer

Heavenly Father,

I affirm that your healing is not dependent on my own strength. I surrender my weaknesses to you and invite you to work in me, bringing healing and restoration. I trust in your power to heal and make me whole. Remind me of your faithfulness when I feel discouraged or overwhelmed. Fill me with hope and confidence in your ability to heal. Thank you for your healing power. I declare that I will rely on you for healing, knowing that your power is made perfect in my weakness. May your healing touch continue to work in me, bringing restoration and wholeness. May your name be glorified.

In Jesus' name, I pray.

Amen.

Day 9: "I affirm that God's healing is a gift of grace. I declare that I will receive His healing with gratitude and allow it to transform my heart and life." (Ephesians 2:8)

Prayer

Heavenly Father,

I receive your healing with gratitude and allow it to transform my heart and life. I surrender myself to your healing grace, recognizing that it is a gift I cannot earn or deserve. Remind me of your faithfulness when doubt or unworthiness arises. Fill me with humility and gratitude for your unmerited favor. Thank you for your healing grace. May your healing power flow through me, bringing transformation and renewal. May your name be glorified.

In Jesus' name, I pray.

Amen.

Day 10: "I affirm that God's healing is a process of forgiveness. I declare that I will choose to forgive those who have hurt me, knowing that forgiveness is a key to healing." (Colossians 3:13)

Prayer

Heavenly Father,

I affirm that your healing is a process of forgiveness. I choose to forgive those who have hurt me, knowing that forgiveness is key to healing. I surrender my hurts and pain to you, asking for your help in releasing bitterness and resentment. Give me strength and grace to forgive, as you have forgiven me. Remind me of your faithfulness when the pain feels overwhelming, or forgiveness seems impossible. Fill me with love and compassion, enabling me to extend forgiveness to others. Thank you for the healing power of forgiveness. May your touch continue to work in my heart, bringing restoration and wholeness. May your name be glorified.

In Jesus' name, I pray.

Amen.

Day 11: "I affirm that God's healing is a journey of faith. I declare that I will trust in His promises and believe that He is able to heal and restore my heart." (Hebrews 11:6)

Prayer

Heavenly Father,

I trust in your promises and believe that you are able to heal and restore my heart. Strengthen my faith and help me to trust in your healing power. Remind me of your faithfulness when doubt or discouragement arises. Fill me with hope and confidence in your ability to heal and restore. Thank you for the journey of faith. May your healing power continue to work in me, bringing transformation and renewal. May your name be glorified.

In Jesus' name, I pray.

Amen.

Day 12: "I affirm that God's healing is a source of hope. I declare that I will hold onto hope, even in the midst of pain, knowing that God is working all things together for my good." (Romans 8:28)

Prayer

Heavenly Father,

I affirm that your healing brings hope. I surrender my pain and struggles to you, inviting you to bring healing to my heart, mind, and body. I choose to hold onto the hope that you are working all things together for my good, even in difficult circumstances. Remind me of your faithfulness when doubt or despair arises. Fill me with steadfast hope and confidence in your plans for my life.

Thank you for the hope that comes through your healing. May your healing power continue to work in me, bringing restoration and wholeness. May your name be glorified.

In Jesus' name, I pray.

Amen.

Day 13: "I affirm that God's healing is a process of surrender. I declare that I will surrender my pain, hurt, and brokenness to Him, allowing Him to heal and restore my heart." (Psalm 55:22)

Prayer

Heavenly Father,

I surrender my pain, hurt, and brokenness to you. I lay down my burdens and invite you to heal and restore my heart. Remind me of your faithfulness when the process feels overwhelming. Fill me with strength and courage to surrender all to you. Thank you for your healing touch. May your power continue to work in me, bringing transformation and renewal. May your name be glorified.

In Jesus' name, I pray.

Amen.

Day 14: "I affirm that God's healing is a result of His compassion and mercy. I declare that He is a compassionate and merciful God, and He desires to heal and comfort me." (Psalm 103:8)

Prayer

Heavenly Father,

I affirm that your healing is a result of your compassion and mercy. I surrender my pain and brokenness to you, inviting you to pour out your compassion and mercy upon me. I trust in your loving kindness and believe that you are able to heal and restore me. Remind me of your compassion and mercy when I feel discouraged or overwhelmed. Fill me with hope and confidence in your ability to heal. Thank you for your compassionate and merciful nature. I trust in your healing power, knowing that it is a result of your compassion and mercy. May your touch continue to work in me, bringing restoration and wholeness. May your name be glorified.

In Jesus' name, I pray.

Amen.

Day 15: "I affirm that God's healing is a journey of transformation. I declare that as He heals my heart, I will be transformed into His likeness, reflecting His love and grace to others." (2 Corinthians 3:18)

Prayer

Heavenly Father,

I surrender myself to your healing touch. Transform me from the inside out so I can reflect your love and grace to others. Remind me of your faithfulness when I feel discouraged. Fill me with a deep desire to be transformed into your likeness. Thank you for the journey of transformation through your healing. May your power continue to work in me, bringing restoration and wholeness. May your name be glorified.

In Jesus' name, I pray.

Amen.

Day 16: "I affirm that God's healing is a process of letting go. I declare that I will let go of bitterness, resentment, and unforgiveness, allowing God's healing to flow freely in my heart." (Ephesians 4:31-32)

Prayer

Heavenly Father,

I surrender my bitterness, resentment, and unforgiveness to you. I release these negative emotions and invite your healing to flow freely in my heart. Remind me of your faithfulness when the pain resurfaces. Fill me with your grace and strength to let go and forgive. Thank you for the healing that comes through letting go. May your touch continue to work in me, bringing restoration and wholeness. May your name be glorified.

In Jesus' name, I pray.

Amen.

Day 17: "I affirm that God's healing is a result of His faithfulness. I declare that He is faithful to His promises, and He will bring healing and restoration to my heart." (Lamentations 3:22-23)

Prayer

Heavenly Father,

I trust in your faithfulness to bring healing and restoration to my heart. I surrender my brokenness and pain to you, knowing that you are able to heal and work all things together for my good. Remind me of your love and mercy when doubt or discouragement arise. Fill me with hope and confidence in your ability to heal. Thank you for your faithfulness. I declare that I will trust in your promises and that your healing power will continue to work in me. May your name be glorified.

In Jesus' name, I pray.

Amen.

Day 18: "I affirm that God's healing is a journey of surrender. I declare that I will surrender my pain, hurt, and brokenness to Him, trusting that He will bring healing and wholeness." (Psalm 147:3)

Prayer

Heavenly Father,

I surrender my pain, hurt, and brokenness to you. I lay down my burdens and invite you to heal and restore my heart. Remind me of your faithfulness when the process feels overwhelming. Fill me with strength and courage to surrender all to you. Thank you for your healing touch. May your power continue to work in me, bringing transformation and renewal. May your name be glorified.

In Jesus' name, I pray.

Amen.

Day 19: "I affirm that God's healing is a process of renewal. I declare that He is renewing my mind, my emotions, and my spirit, bringing healing and transformation to every area of my life." (Romans 12:2)

Prayer

Heavenly Father,

I surrender myself to your renewing touch. Transform my mind, emotions, and spirit, bringing healing and transformation to every area of my life. Remind me of your faithfulness when the process feels challenging. Fill me with strength and perseverance to continue on this journey of healing. Thank you for your healing and renewing power. May your touch continue to work in me, bringing restoration and wholeness. May your name be glorified.

In Jesus' name, I pray.

Amen.

Day 20: "I affirm that God's healing is a result of His love and compassion. I declare that His love is unfailing, and His compassion is endless, bringing healing and restoration to my heart." (Psalm 86:15)

Prayer

Heavenly Father,

I surrender my heart to your love and compassion. Pour out your healing touch upon me. I trust in your unfailing love and believe that you can bring restoration and wholeness to every area of my life. Remind me of your love and compassion when I feel discouraged or overwhelmed. Fill me with hope and confidence in your ability to heal. Thank you for your love and compassion. I declare that I will trust in your healing power, knowing that it is a result of your unfailing love and endless compassion. May your healing touch continue to work in me, bringing restoration and wholeness. May your name be glorified.

In Jesus' name, I pray.

Amen.

Day 21: "I affirm that God's healing is a journey of trust. I declare that I will trust in His goodness and His plans for my life, knowing that He is working all things for my ultimate healing and wholeness." (Proverbs 3:5-6)

Amen.

Prayer

Heavenly Father,

I trust in your goodness and your plans for my life. I surrender my doubts and fears to you, choosing to trust in your wisdom and guidance. I believe that you have a purpose and a plan for me, and I trust that you are leading me toward healing and wholeness. Remind me of your faithfulness when doubt or fear arise. Fill me with a deep sense of trust in your love and provision. Thank you for the journey of trust in your healing. May your healing power continue to work in me, bringing restoration and transformation. May your name be glorified.

In Jesus' name, I pray.

Amen.

Day 22: "I affirm that God's healing is a process of surrender. I declare that I will surrender my pain, hurt, and brokenness to Him, allowing Him to heal and restore my heart." (Psalm 55:22)

Prayer

Heavenly Father,

I surrender my pain, hurt, and brokenness to you. Heal and restore my heart. Remind me of your faithfulness when the process feels overwhelming. Fill me with strength and courage to surrender all to you. Thank you for the process of surrender and healing. May your healing power continue to work in me, bringing transformation and renewal. May your name be glorified.

In Jesus' name, I pray.

Amen.

Day 23: "I affirm that God's healing is a result of His grace. I declare that His grace is sufficient for me, and His power is made perfect in my weakness, bringing healing and restoration to my heart." (2 Corinthians 12:9)

Prayer

Heavenly Father,

Your grace brings healing and restoration to my heart. I surrender my weaknesses and limitations to you, knowing that your power is made perfect in my weakness. Remind me of your grace when I feel inadequate or overwhelmed. Fill me with a deep sense of your love and grace, knowing that you are working in and through me to bring healing and renewal. Thank you for your grace. May your healing power continue to work in me, bringing transformation and renewal. May your name be glorified.

In Jesus' name, I pray.

Amen.

Day 24: "I affirm that God's healing is a journey of transformation. I declare that as He heals my heart, I will be transformed into His likeness, reflecting His love and grace to others." (2 Corinthians 3:18)

Prayer

Heavenly Father,

I surrender myself to your transformative touch. Bring healing and restoration to my heart. Transform me into your likeness, reflecting your love and grace to others. Remind me of your faithfulness when the journey feels challenging. Fill me with strength and perseverance to continue on this journey of healing and transformation. Thank you for the journey of transformation through your healing. May your transformative touch continue to work in me, bringing restoration and renewal. May your name be glorified.

In Jesus' name, I pray.

Amen.

Day 25: "I affirm that God's healing is a process of forgiveness. I declare that I will choose to forgive those who have hurt me, knowing that forgiveness is a key to healing." (Colossians 3:13)

Prayer

Heavenly Father,

I choose to forgive those who have hurt me, knowing that forgiveness is a key to healing. I release any bitterness, resentment, or anger that I may be holding onto. Help me to let go of grudges and negative emotions. Remind me of your grace and mercy when forgiveness feels difficult. Fill me with your love and compassion, enabling me to extend forgiveness to others. Thank you for the process of forgiveness and healing. May your healing power continue to work in me, bringing restoration and wholeness. May your name be glorified.

In Jesus' name, I pray.

Amen.

Day 26: "I affirm that God's healing is a journey of faith. I declare that I will trust in His promises and believe that He is able to heal and restore my heart." (Hebrews 11:6)

Prayer

Heavenly Father,

I trust in your promises and believe that you are able to heal and restore my heart. I surrender my doubts and fears to you, choosing to trust in your faithfulness. Remind me of your power and love when my faith wavers. Fill me with a deep sense of faith and confidence in your ability to heal. Thank you for the journey of faith in your healing. May your healing power continue to work in me, bringing transformation and renewal. May your name be glorified.

In Jesus' name, I pray.

Amen.

Day 27: "I affirm that God's healing is a source of hope. I declare that I will hold onto hope, even in the midst of pain, knowing that God is working all things together for my good." (Romans 8:28)

Prayer

Heavenly Father,

I hold onto hope, even in the midst of pain, knowing that you are working all things together for my good. I surrender my pain and struggles to you, placing my hope in your ability to bring beauty out of ashes. Remind me of your faithfulness when hope feels distant. Fill me with a deep sense of hope and assurance in your love and provision. Thank you for the source of hope that comes through your healing. May your healing power continue to work in me, bringing transformation and renewal. May your name be glorified.

In Jesus' name, I pray.

Amen.

Day 28: "I affirm that God's healing is a process of surrender. I declare that I will surrender my pain, hurt, and brokenness to Him, allowing Him to heal and restore my heart." (Psalm 55:22)

Prayer

Heavenly Father,

I surrender my pain, hurt, and brokenness to you. I lay down my burdens at your feet, knowing that you are able to bear them for me. I trust that you can bring wholeness and restoration. Remind me of your presence and faithfulness when the process feels overwhelming. Fill me with surrender and trust in your healing power. Thank you for the process of surrender and healing. May your healing power continue to work in me, bringing transformation and renewal. May your name be glorified.

In Jesus' name, I pray.

Amen.

Day 29: "I affirm that God's healing is a result of His compassion and mercy. I declare that He is a compassionate and merciful God, and He desires to heal and comfort me." (Psalm 103:8)

Prayer

Heavenly Father,

I thank you for your compassion and mercy that knows no bounds. I surrender my hurts and wounds to you, knowing that you are able to heal and restore. Remind me of your compassion and mercy when I feel overwhelmed or discouraged. Fill me with a deep sense of your compassion and mercy, knowing that you are near to the brokenhearted. Thank you for the healing that comes through your compassion and mercy. May your healing power continue to work in me, bringing transformation and renewal. May your name be glorified.

In Jesus' name, I pray.

Amen.

Day 30: "I affirm that God's healing is a journey of transformation. I declare that as He heals my heart, I will be transformed into His likeness, reflecting His love and grace to others." (2 Corinthians 3:18)

Prayer

Heavenly Father,

I surrender myself to your transformative touch. Heal the broken places in my heart and bring restoration and renewal to every area of my life. Transform me into your likeness so I may reflect your love and grace to others. Remind me of your faithfulness when the journey feels challenging. Fill me with strength and perseverance to continue on this journey of healing and transformation. Thank you for the journey of transformation through your healing. May your transformative touch continue to work in me, bringing restoration and renewal. May your name be glorified.

In Jesus' name, I pray.

Amen.

Day 31: "I affirm that God's healing is a process of letting go. I declare that I will let go of bitterness, resentment, and unforgiveness, allowing God's healing to flow freely in my heart." (Ephesians 4:31-32

Prayer

Heavenly Father,

I surrender my bitterness, resentment, and unforgiveness to you. I choose to let go and forgive, knowing that forgiveness is a key to healing. Help me release these burdens and replace them with your love and peace. Remind me of your grace and mercy when letting go feels difficult. Fill me with your love and compassion, enabling me to let go and forgive. Thank you for the process of letting go and healing. May your healing power continue to work in me, bringing restoration and wholeness. May your name be glorified.

In Jesus' name, I pray.

Amen.

STRENGTH TO MOVE ON

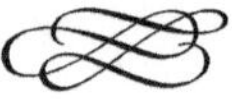

Day 1: "I affirm that God is my strength and my refuge. He gives me the power to move on and face each day with courage and determination." (Psalm 18:2)

Prayer

Heavenly Father,

You are my strength and refuge. I thank you for empowering me to face each day with courage and determination. I surrender my weaknesses and insecurities to you, asking for your strength to fill me. Help me trust in your unfailing love and lean on you in difficult times. Remind me of your presence and power when I feel weak or discouraged. Fill me with your strength and courage, knowing that I can do all things through Christ who strengthens me. Thank you for being my strength and refuge.

May your name be glorified.

In Jesus' name, I pray.

Amen.

Day 2: "I affirm that God's grace is sufficient for me. In my weakness, His strength is made perfect, and I can do all things through Christ who strengthens me." (2 Corinthians 12:9, Philippians 4:13)

Prayer

Heavenly Father,

Your grace is sufficient for me. In my weakness, your strength is made perfect, and I can do all things through Christ who strengthens me. I surrender my weaknesses and limitations to you, knowing that with your strength, I can accomplish all that you have called me to do. Fill me with your empowering grace, enabling me to walk in victory and fulfill your purposes for my life. Remind me of your all-sufficient grace when I feel inadequate or overwhelmed. Help me to hold onto the truth that your strength is made perfect in my weakness. Thank you for your abundant grace and the strength that comes through Christ. May your grace continue to empower me, bringing glory to your name. In Jesus' name, I pray.

Amen.

Day 3: "I affirm that God is my rock and my fortress. He is my stronghold in times of trouble, and I find refuge in Him." (Psalm 18:2)

Prayer

Heavenly Father,

You are my rock and fortress, my place of safety. I surrender my fears and anxieties to you, asking for your protection and guidance. Help me trust in your unfailing love and find comfort in your presence. Remind me of your faithfulness when I feel overwhelmed. Fill me with your peace and security, knowing that I am safe in your hands. Thank you for being my rock and fortress. May your presence bring peace and protection. May your name be glorified.

In Jesus' name, I pray.

Amen.

Day 4: "I affirm that God is my helper. He upholds me with His righteous right hand and gives me the strength to overcome any obstacle." (Isaiah 41:10)

Prayer

Heavenly Father,

You are my helper, upholding me with your righteous right hand. I surrender my weaknesses and limitations to you, knowing that with your help, I can conquer any obstacle. Give me strength and guidance in difficult times.

Remind me of your promise to be my helper and fill me with your strength and courage. Thank you for being my helper. With your strength, I can overcome any obstacle. May your presence uphold me and bring glory to your name.

In Jesus' name, I pray.

Amen.

Day 5: "I affirm that God is my peace. In His presence, I find rest and tranquility, even in the midst of challenges and uncertainties." (Philippians 4:7)

Prayer

Heavenly Father,

You are my peace. In your presence, I find rest and tranquility, even in the midst of challenges and uncertainties. I surrender my worries and anxieties to you, knowing that you are in control and have a plan for my life. Help me trust in your unfailing love and find peace in your presence. Remind me of your peace that surpasses all understanding when I feel overwhelmed or anxious. Fill me with a deep sense of your peace and tranquility, knowing that I am safe in your hands. Thank you for being my peace. May your peace continue to guard my heart and mind in Christ Jesus.

May your name be glorified.

In Jesus' name, I pray.

Amen.

Day 6: "I affirm that God is my provider. He meets all my needs according to His riches in glory, and He will never leave me lacking." (Philippians 4:19)

Prayer

Heavenly Father,

You are my provider. I trust in your unfailing love and provision for my life. Help me to rely on you and not on my own understanding. Remind me of your promise to provide for me and fill me with trust and confidence in your provision. Thank you for being my provider. I declare that I trust in your provision and rely on your faithfulness. May your provision continue to manifest in my life, bringing glory to your name.

In Jesus' name, I pray.

Amen.

Day 7: "I affirm that God is my refuge and strength, a very present help in times of trouble. I find comfort and strength in His presence, knowing that He will never leave me nor forsake me." (Psalm 46:1)

Prayer

Heavenly Father,

You are my refuge and strength. I surrender my troubles and burdens to you, knowing that you can carry them and provide me with the strength I need. Help me trust in your unfailing love and find refuge in your presence. Remind me that you are always with me, guiding and protecting me. Fill me with your presence and peace, knowing that I am safe in your hands. Thank you for being my refuge and strength. I find comfort and strength in your presence, and I trust in your unfailing love. May your name be glorified.

In Jesus' name, I pray.

Amen.

Day 8: "I affirm that God is my guide. He leads me on the path of righteousness and directs my steps in the way I should go." (Psalm 32:8)

Prayer

Heavenly Father,

You are my guide. I surrender my plans and desires to you, trusting in your higher ways and thoughts. Help me to trust in your guidance and follow your leading in every aspect of my life. Remind me of your promise to never leave me and to guide me with your eye upon me. Fill me with your presence and peace, knowing that I am on the right path with you as my guide. Thank you for being my guide. I trust in your guidance and rely on your wisdom. May your name be glorified in all that I do.

In Jesus' name, I pray.

Amen.

Day 9: "I affirm that God is my restorer. He restores my soul and brings beauty from ashes." (Psalm 23:3)

Prayer

Heavenly Father,

You are my restorer. I surrender my brokenness and pain to you, knowing that you can heal and restore. Help me trust in your unfailing love and find comfort in your presence. Remind me of your promise to restore my soul and bring beauty from ashes. Fill me with a deep sense of your restoration and healing. Thank you for being my restorer. I trust in your restoration and rely on your faithfulness. May your name be glorified in all that I do.

In Jesus' name, I pray.

Amen.

Day 10: "I affirm that God is my peace. He gives me peace that surpasses all understanding, even in the midst of challenges and uncertainties." (Philippians 4:7)

Prayer

Heavenly Father,

You are my peace. I surrender my worries and anxieties to you, knowing that you are in control and have a plan for my life. Help me trust in your unfailing love and find peace in your presence. Remind me of your promise to be my peace and fill me with a deep sense of tranquility. Thank you for being my peace. May your peace continue to guard my heart and mind in Christ Jesus. May your name be glorified.

In Jesus' name, I pray.

Amen.

Day 11: "I affirm that God is my refuge and strength, a very present help in times of trouble. I find comfort and strength in His presence, knowing that He will never leave me nor forsake me." (Psalm 46:1)

Prayer

Heavenly Father,

You are my refuge and strength. I surrender my troubles and burdens to you, knowing that you can carry them and provide me with the strength I need. Help me trust in your unfailing love and find refuge in your presence. Remind me of your promise to be with me, guiding and protecting me. Fill me with your presence and peace, knowing that I am safe in your hands. Thank you for being my refuge and strength. I find comfort and strength in your presence, and I trust in your unfailing love. May your name be glorified.

In Jesus' name, I pray.

Amen.

Day 12: "I affirm that God is my helper. He upholds me with His righteous right hand and gives me the strength to overcome any obstacle." (Isaiah 41:10)

Prayer

Heavenly Father,

You are my helper. I surrender my weaknesses and challenges to you, knowing that you provide the strength and help I need. Help me trust in your unfailing love and rely on your guidance. Remind me of your promise to uphold me and give me the strength to overcome. Fill me with your presence and power, knowing that I can do all things through Christ who strengthens me. Thank you for being my helper. I trust in your strength and righteousness. May your help continue to manifest in my life, bringing glory to your name.

In Jesus' name, I pray.

Amen.

Day 13: "I affirm that God is my rock and my fortress. He is my stronghold in times of trouble, and I find refuge in Him." (Psalm 18:2)

Prayer

Heavenly Father,

You are my rock and fortress. I surrender my troubles and fears to you, knowing that you can protect and provide for me. Help me trust in your unfailing love and find refuge in your presence. Remind me of your promise to be my stronghold in times of trouble. Fill me with your presence and peace, knowing that I am safe in your hands. Thank you for being my rock and fortress. I find strength and security in your presence, and I trust in your unfailing love. May your name be glorified.

In Jesus' name, I pray.

Amen.

Day 14: "I affirm that God is my provider. He meets all my needs according to His riches in glory, and He will never leave me lacking." (Philippians 4:19)

Prayer

Heavenly Father,

You are my provider. I surrender my worries and concerns about provision to you, knowing that you are able to provide abundantly. Help me trust in your unfailing love and rely on your provision. Remind me of your promise to meet all my needs according to your riches in glory. Thank you for being my provider. I trust in your provision and rely on your abundance. May your provision continue to manifest in my life, bringing glory to your name.

In Jesus' name, I pray.

Amen.

Day 15: "I affirm that God is my strength and my shield. He gives me the strength to persevere through difficult times and protects me from harm." (Psalm 28:7)

Prayer

Heavenly Father,

You are my strength and shield. I surrender my weaknesses and vulnerabilities to you, knowing that you can strengthen me and protect me. Help me trust in your unfailing love and rely on your strength. Remind me of your promise to be my strength and shield. Fill me with your strength and protection, knowing that I am safe in your hands. Thank you for being my strength and shield. I trust in your strength and rely on your protection. May your name be glorified.

In Jesus' name, I pray.

Amen.

Day 16: "I affirm that God is my comforter. He comforts me in all my troubles, and His peace surpasses all understanding." (2 Corinthians 1:3-4)

Prayer

Heavenly Father,

You are my comforter. I surrender my troubles and sorrows to you, knowing that you can bring me comfort and peace. Help me trust in your unfailing love and find solace in your presence. Remind me of your promise to be near to the brokenhearted. Fill me with your comfort and peace, knowing that I am held in your loving arms. Thank you for being my comforter. I find solace and peace in your presence, and I trust in your unfailing love. May your comfort continue to envelop me, and your peace surpasses all understanding. May your name be glorified.

In Jesus' name, I pray.

Amen.

Day 17: "I affirm that God is my guide. He leads me on the path of righteousness and directs my steps in the way I should go." (Psalm 32:8)

Prayer

Heavenly Father,

You are my guide. I surrender my plans and decisions to you, knowing that you can lead me in the right direction. Help me trust in your unfailing love and follow your leading. Remind me of your promise to guide me on the path of righteousness. Fill me with your guidance and wisdom, knowing that I can trust in your perfect plan for my life. Thank you for being my guide. I trust in your guidance and rely on your wisdom. May your name be glorified.

In Jesus' name, I pray.

Amen.

Day 18: "I affirm that God is my restorer. He restores my soul and brings beauty from ashes." (Psalm 23:3)

Prayer

Heavenly Father,

You are my restorer. I surrender my brokenness and pain to you, knowing that you can restore and heal my soul. Help me trust in your unfailing love and find solace in your restoration. Remind me of your promise to bring beauty from ashes. Fill me with a deep sense of your restoration and renewal, knowing that you can bring beauty from the ashes of my life. Thank you for being my restorer. I trust in your restoration and rely on your healing power. May your restoration continue to work in my life, bringing beauty and wholeness. May your name be glorified.

In Jesus' name, I pray.

Amen.

Day 19: "I affirm that God is my peace. He gives me peace that surpasses all understanding, even in the midst of challenges and uncertainties." (Philippians 4:7)

Prayer

Heavenly Father,

You are my peace. I surrender my worries and anxieties to you, knowing that you can calm my troubled heart and bring peace to my soul. Help me trust in your unfailing love and find rest in your peace. Remind me of your promise to be my peace, even in moments of chaos and confusion. Fill me with a deep sense of your peace, knowing that I can trust in your sovereignty and control. Thank you for being my peace. I find rest and tranquility in your presence, and I trust in your unfailing love. May your peace continue to guard my heart and mind, surpassing all understanding. May your name be glorified.

In Jesus' name, I pray.

Amen.

Day 20: "I affirm that God is my refuge and strength, a very present help in times of trouble. I find comfort and strength in His presence, knowing that He will never leave me nor forsake me." (Psalm 46:1)

Prayer

Heavenly Father,

You are my refuge and strength. I surrender my troubles and burdens to you, knowing that you can provide refuge and strength in any situation. Help me trust in your unfailing love and find solace in your presence. Remind me of your promise to be with me in times of trouble. Fill me with a deep sense of your presence, knowing that I can find rest and peace in you. Thank you for being my refuge and strength. I trust in your provision and rely on your power. May your name be glorified.

In Jesus' name, I pray.

Amen.

Day 21: "I affirm that God is my helper. He upholds me with His righteous right hand and gives me the strength to overcome any obstacle." (Isaiah 41:10)

Prayer

Heavenly Father,

You are my helper. I surrender my weaknesses and limitations to you, knowing that you can give me the strength I need. Help me trust in your unfailing love and rely on your power. Remind me of your promise to be with me in difficult times. Fill me with your strength and assistance, knowing that I can overcome any obstacle with you by my side. Thank you for being my helper. I trust in your assistance and rely on your strength. May your help continue to empower me, and may your name be glorified.

In Jesus' name, I pray.

Amen.

Day 22: "I affirm that God is my rock and my fortress. He is my stronghold in times of trouble, and I find refuge in Him." (Psalm 18:2)

Prayer

Heavenly Father,

You are my rock and fortress. I surrender my fears and anxieties to you, knowing that you provide strength and protection. Help me trust in your unfailing love and find security in your presence. Remind me of your promise to be my stronghold in times of trouble. Fill me with a deep sense of your presence, knowing that I can find refuge and peace in you. Thank you for being my rock and fortress. I trust in your strength and rely on your protection. May your name be glorified.

In Jesus' name, I pray.

Amen.

Day 23: "I affirm that God is my provider. He meets all my needs according to His riches in glory, and He will never leave me lacking." (Philippians 4:19)

Prayer

Heavenly Father,

You are my provider. I surrender my worries and concerns about provision to you, knowing that you can abundantly provide and sustain me in every season of life. Help me trust in your unfailing love and rely on your provision. Remind me of your promise to be my provider, even in moments of uncertainty and lack. Fill me with a deep sense of your provision and abundance, knowing that I can trust in your faithfulness. Thank you for being my provider. I trust in your provision and rely on your abundance. May your name be glorified.

In Jesus' name, I pray.

Amen.

Day 24: "I affirm that God is my strength and my shield. He gives me the strength to persevere through difficult times and protects me from harm." (Psalm 28:7)

Prayer

Heavenly Father,

You are my strength and shield. I surrender my weaknesses and vulnerabilities to you, knowing that you can strengthen me and protect me from harm. Help me trust in your unfailing love and find courage in your presence. Remind me of your promise to be my strength and shield, especially in moments of weakness and danger. Fill me with a deep sense of your strength and protection, knowing that I can face any challenge with you by my side. Thank you for being my strength and shield. I trust in your power and rely on your protection. May your name be glorified.

In Jesus' name, I pray.

Amen.

Day 25: "I affirm that God is my comforter. He comforts me in all my troubles, and His peace surpasses all understanding." (2 Corinthians 1:3-4)

Prayer

Heavenly Father,

You are my comforter. I surrender my troubles and burdens to you, knowing that you can bring comfort and peace to my soul. Help me trust in your unfailing love and find solace in your presence. Remind me of your promise to be my comforter, especially in moments of distress and sorrow. Fill me with a deep sense of your presence, knowing that I can find rest and tranquility in you. Thank you for being my comforter. I find comfort and peace in your presence, and I trust in your unfailing love. May your peace continue to guard my heart and mind, surpassing all understanding.

May your name be glorified.

In Jesus' name, I pray.

Amen.

Day 26: "I affirm that God is my guide. He leads me on the path of righteousness and directs my steps in the way I should go." (Psalm 32:8)

Prayer

Heavenly Father,

You are my guide. I surrender my plans and decisions to you, knowing that you can lead me in the right direction. Help me trust in your unfailing love and seek your guidance in all that I do. Remind me of your promise to lead me on the path of righteousness. Fill me with a deep sense of your guidance and direction, knowing that I can trust in your wisdom and understanding. Thank you for being my guide. I trust in your leading and rely on your direction. May your guidance continue to illuminate my path, and may your name be glorified.

In Jesus' name, I pray.

Amen.

Day 27: "I affirm that God is my restorer. He restores my soul and brings beauty from ashes." (Psalm 23:3)

Prayer

Heavenly Father,

You are my restorer. I surrender my brokenness and pain to you, knowing that you can restore my soul and bring healing to my wounds. Help me trust in your unfailing love and find comfort in your presence. Remind me of your promise to be my restorer, especially in moments of despair and brokenness. Fill me with a deep sense of your restoration and renewal, knowing that I can find hope and healing in you. Thank you for being my restorer. I trust in your restoration and rely on your healing. May your restoration continue to bring beauty to my life, and may your name be glorified.

In Jesus' name, I pray.

Amen.

Day 28: "I affirm that God is my peace. He gives me peace that surpasses all understanding, even in the midst of challenges and uncertainties." (Philippians 4:7)

Prayer

Heavenly Father,

You are my peace. I surrender my worries and anxieties to you, knowing that you can calm my heart and bring peace to my soul. Help me trust in your unfailing love and find rest in your presence. Remind me of your promise to be my peace, especially in moments of chaos and confusion.

Fill me with a deep sense of your peace, knowing that I can find serenity and calmness in you. Thank you for being my peace. I trust in your peace and rely on your tranquility. May your peace continue to guard my heart and mind, surpassing all understanding. May your name be glorified.

In Jesus' name, I pray.

Amen.

Day 29: "I affirm that God is my refuge and strength, a very present help in times of trouble. I find comfort and strength in His presence, knowing that He will never leave me nor forsake me." (Psalm 46:1)

Prayer

Heavenly Father,

You are my refuge and strength. I surrender my troubles and fears to you, knowing that you can provide refuge and strength in any storm. Help me trust in your unfailing love and find solace in your presence. Remind me of your promise to be my refuge and strength, especially in times of trouble and uncertainty. Fill me with a deep sense of your presence, knowing that I can find safety and strength in you. Thank you for being my refuge and strength. I trust in your provision and rely on your power.

May your presence continue to be my source of comfort and strength. May your name be glorified.

In Jesus' name, I pray.

Amen.

Day 30: "I affirm that God is my helper. He upholds me with His righteous right hand and gives me the strength to overcome any obstacle." (Isaiah 41:10)

Prayer

Heavenly Father,

You are my helper. I surrender my weaknesses and limitations to you, knowing that you can lift me up and empower me to overcome any challenge. Help me trust in your unfailing love and find courage in your presence. Remind me of your promise to be my helper, upholding me with your righteous right hand. Fill me with a deep sense of your strength and empowerment, knowing that I can overcome any obstacle with you by my side. Thank you for being my helper. I trust in your strength and rely on your guidance. May your power continue to work in me, enabling me to overcome every obstacle. May your name be glorified.

In Jesus' name, I pray.

Amen.

Day 31: "I affirm that God is my source of hope. In Him, I find strength and courage to face each day with confidence, knowing that He has a plan and purpose for my life." (Jeremiah 29:11)

Prayer

Heavenly Father,

You are my source of hope. I surrender my doubts and fears to you, knowing that you can fill me with hope and confidence. Help me trust in your unfailing love and find assurance in your promises. Remind me of your plan and purpose for my life, especially in moments of uncertainty and confusion. Fill me with your strength and courage so that I can face each day with confidence. Thank you for being my source of hope. I trust in your plans and rely on your guidance. May your hope continue to fill my heart, and may your name be glorified.

In Jesus' name, I pray.

Amen.

EMOTIONAL HEALING

Day 1: "I affirm that God is my healer. He binds up my wounds and brings emotional healing to my heart and mind." (Psalm 147:3)

Prayer

Heavenly Father,

I come before you today, affirming that you are my healer. Your Word assures me that you bind up my wounds and bring emotional healing to my heart and mind. I thank you for your faithfulness in being my source of healing and restoration.

Lord, I surrender my hurts and pains to you. I lay them at your feet, knowing that you are able to bring healing and wholeness to every area of my life. Help me to trust in your unfailing love and to find comfort in your presence.

Father, in moments of brokenness and emotional turmoil, remind me of your promise to be my healer. Help me to hold onto the truth that you are always with me, bringing healing and restoration. Fill me with a deep sense of your healing power, knowing that you can mend my wounds and bring emotional healing to my heart and mind.

Thank you, Lord, for being my healer. I declare that I trust in your healing and rely on your restoration. May your healing continue to bring wholeness to my life, and may your name be glorified in all that I do.

In Jesus' name, I pray.

Amen.

Day 2: "I affirm that God is my comforter. He comforts me in all my sorrows and brings peace to my troubled soul." (2 Corinthians 1:3-4)

Prayer

Heavenly Father,

I come before you today, affirming that you are my comforter. Your Word assures me that you are the God of all comfort, who comforts me in all my sorrows and brings peace to my troubled soul. I thank you for your faithfulness in being my source of comfort and solace.

Lord, I surrender my sorrows and troubles to you. I lay them at your feet, knowing that you are able to bring comfort and peace to my troubled soul. Help me to trust in your unfailing love and to find rest in your presence.

Father, in moments of sadness and distress, remind me of your promise to be my comforter. Help me to hold onto the truth that you are always with me, offering comfort and peace. Fill me with a deep sense of your comforting presence, knowing that I can find solace and tranquility in you.

Thank you, Lord, for being my comforter. I declare that I trust in your comfort and rely on your peace. May your comfort continue to bring healing to my soul, and may your name be glorified in all that I do.

In Jesus' name, I pray.

Amen.

Day 3: "I affirm that God is my refuge. In Him, I find safety and security, and He shields me from emotional pain." (Psalm 46:1)

Prayer

Heavenly Father,

I come before you today, affirming that you are my refuge. In you, I find safety and security, and you shield me from emotional pain. Your Word assures me that you are a strong tower, a place of refuge in times of trouble. I thank you for your faithfulness in being my source of protection and comfort.

Lord, I surrender my fears and anxieties to you. I lay them at your feet, knowing that you are able to provide refuge and peace in the midst of any storm. Help me to trust in your unfailing love and to find solace in your presence.

Father, in moments of emotional pain and distress, remind me of your promise to be my refuge. Help me to hold onto the truth that you are always with me, shielding me from harm. Fill me with a deep sense of your presence, knowing that I can find safety and security in you.

Thank you, Lord, for being my refuge. I declare that I trust in your protection and rely on your comfort. May your refuge continue to be my place of safety, and may your name be glorified in all that I do.

In Jesus' name, I pray.

Amen.

Day 4: "I affirm that God is my strength. He gives me the strength to overcome emotional challenges and empowers me to move forward." (Philippians 4:13)

Prayer

Heavenly Father,

I come before you today, affirming that you are my strength. Your Word assures me that I can do all things through Christ who strengthens me. I thank you for your faithfulness in being my source of strength and empowerment.

Lord, I surrender my emotional challenges to you. I lay them at your feet, knowing that you are able to give me the strength to overcome them. Help me to trust in your unfailing love and to find courage in your presence.

Father, in moments of weakness and discouragement, remind me of your promise to be my strength. Help me to hold onto the truth that I can do all things through Christ who strengthens me. Fill me with a deep sense of your strength and empowerment, knowing that I can move forward with confidence because of you.

Thank you, Lord, for being my strength. I declare that I trust in your power and rely on your guidance. May your strength continue to empower me to overcome every emotional challenge that comes my way. May your name be glorified in all that I do.

In Jesus' name, I pray.

Amen.

Day 5: "I affirm that God is my peace. In His presence, I find rest and tranquility, even in the midst of emotional turmoil." (Philippians 4:7)

Prayer

Heavenly Father,

I come before you today, affirming that you are my peace. In your presence, I find rest and tranquility, even in the midst of emotional turmoil. Your Word assures me that when I bring my anxieties to you in Prayer, your peace, which surpasses all understanding, will guard my heart and mind in Christ Jesus.

Lord, I surrender my worries and anxieties to you. I lay them at your feet, knowing that you are able to bring peace and calm to my troubled soul. Help me to trust in your unfailing love and to find solace in your presence.

Father, in moments of emotional turmoil and unrest, remind me of your promise to be my peace. Help me to hold onto the truth that your peace surpasses all understanding and can guard my heart and mind. Fill me with a deep sense of your peace, knowing that I can find rest and tranquility in you.

Thank you, Lord, for being my peace. I declare that I trust in your peace and rely on your presence. May your peace continue to calm my troubled soul, and may your name be glorified in all that I do.

In Jesus' name, I pray.

Amen.

Day 6: "I affirm that God is my hope. In Him, I find the assurance that He will restore and renew my emotional well-being." (Jeremiah 29:11)

Prayer

Heavenly Father,

I come before you today, affirming that you are my hope. In you, I find the assurance that you will restore and renew my emotional well-being. Your Word assures me that you have plans for my life, plans to prosper me and not to harm me, plans to give me hope and a future. I thank you for your faithfulness in being my source of hope and restoration.

Lord, I surrender my emotional struggles to you. I lay them at your feet, knowing that you are able to bring restoration and renewal to my well-being. Help me to trust in your unfailing love and to find comfort in your presence.

Father, in moments of despair and uncertainty, remind me of your promise to restore and renew me. Help me to hold onto the truth that you have plans for my life, plans that bring hope and a future. Fill me with a deep sense of your hope, knowing that you are working all things together for my good.

Thank you, Lord, for being my hope. I declare that I trust in your plans and rely on your restoration. May your hope continue to fill my heart, and may your name be glorified in all that I do.

In Jesus' name, I pray.

Amen.

Day 7: "I affirm that God is my healer. He heals the brokenhearted and binds up their wounds." (Psalm 147:3)

Prayer

Heavenly Father,

I come before you today, affirming that you are my healer. Your Word assures me that you heal the brokenhearted and bind up their wounds. I thank you for your faithfulness in being my source of healing and restoration.

Lord, I surrender my brokenness and pain to you. I lay them at your feet, knowing that you are able to bring healing and wholeness to every area of my life. Help me to trust in your unfailing love and to find comfort in your presence.

Father, in moments of emotional turmoil and distress, remind me of your promise to be my healer. Help me to hold onto the truth that you can mend my wounds and bring emotional healing to my heart and mind. Fill me with a deep sense of your healing power, knowing that you can restore and renew me.

Thank you, Lord, for being my healer. I declare that I trust in your healing and rely on your restoration. May your healing continue to bring wholeness to my life, and may your name be glorified in all that I do.

In Jesus' name, I pray.

Amen.

Day 8: "I affirm that God is my comforter. He comforts me in all my afflictions and brings solace to my soul." (2 Corinthians 1:3-4)

Prayer

Heavenly Father,

I come before you today, affirming that you are my comforter. Your Word assures me that you are the God of all comfort, who comforts me in all my afflictions and brings solace to my soul. I thank you for your faithfulness in being my source of comfort and peace.

Lord, I surrender my afflictions and troubles to you. I lay them at your feet, knowing that you are able to bring comfort and solace to my troubled soul. Help me to trust in your unfailing love and to find rest in your presence.

Father, in moments of sadness and distress, remind me of your promise to be my comforter. Help me to hold onto the truth that you are always with me, offering comfort and peace. Fill me with a deep sense of your comforting presence, knowing that I can find solace and tranquility in you.

Thank you, Lord, for being my comforter. I declare that I trust in your comfort and rely on your peace. May your comfort continue to bring healing to my soul, and may your name be glorified in all that I do.

In Jesus' name, I pray.

Amen.

Day 9: "I affirm that God is my refuge. In Him, I find shelter and protection from emotional storms." (Psalm 46:1)

Prayer

Heavenly Father,

I come before you today, affirming that you are my refuge. In you, I find shelter and protection from the emotional storms that surround me. Your Word assures me that you are a strong tower, a place of safety and security. I thank you for your faithfulness in being my source of refuge and strength.

Lord, I surrender my fears and anxieties to you. I lay them at your feet, knowing that you are able to provide refuge and peace in the midst of any storm. Help me to trust in your unfailing love and to find solace in your presence.

Father, in moments of emotional turmoil and distress, remind me of your promise to be my refuge. Help me to hold onto the truth that you are always with me, shielding me from harm. Fill me with a deep sense of your presence, knowing that I can find safety and security in you.

Thank you, Lord, for being my refuge. I declare that I trust in your protection and rely on your comfort. May your refuge continue to be my place of safety, and may your name be glorified in all that I do.

In Jesus' name, I pray.

Amen.

Day 10: "I affirm that God is my strength. He strengthens me in my weakness and gives me the power to overcome emotional challenges." (Philippians 4:13)

Prayer

Heavenly Father,

I come before you today, affirming that you are my strength. Your Word assures me that I can do all things through Christ who strengthens me. I thank you for your faithfulness in being my source of strength and empowerment.

Lord, I surrender my emotional challenges to you. I lay them at your feet, knowing that you can give me the strength to overcome them. Help me to trust in your unfailing love and to find courage in your presence.

Father, in moments of weakness and struggle, remind me of your promise to strengthen me. Help me to hold onto the truth that I can do all things through Christ, who empowers me. Fill me with a deep sense of your strength, knowing that I am not alone in my battles.

Thank you, Lord, for being my strength. I declare that I trust in your power and rely on your guidance. May your strength continue to empower me to overcome every emotional challenge. May your name be glorified in all that I do.

In Jesus' name, I pray.

Amen.

Day 11: "I affirm that God is my peace. In His presence, I find serenity and calmness, even in the midst of emotional turmoil." (Philippians 4:7)

Prayer

Heavenly Father,

I come before you today, affirming that you are my peace. In your presence, I find serenity and calmness, even in the midst of emotional turmoil. Your Word assures me that your peace surpasses all understanding and can guard my heart and mind. I thank you for your faithfulness in being my source of peace and tranquility.

Lord, I surrender my worries and anxieties to you. I lay them at your feet, knowing that you can bring calm to my troubled soul. Help me to trust in your unfailing love and to find solace in your presence.

Father, in moments of emotional turmoil and distress, remind me of your promise to be my peace. Help me to hold onto the truth that your peace surpasses all understanding and can guard my heart and mind. Fill me with a deep sense of your peace, knowing that I can find rest and tranquility in you.

Thank you, Lord, for being my peace. I declare that I trust in your peace and rely on your presence. May your peace continue to calm my troubled soul, and may your name be glorified in all that I do.

In Jesus' name, I pray.

Amen.

Day 12: "I affirm that God is my hope. In Him, I find the assurance that He will restore and renew my emotional well-being." (Jeremiah 29:11)

Prayer

Heavenly Father,

I come before you today, affirming that you are my hope. In you, I find the assurance that you will restore and renew my emotional well-being. Your Word assures me that you have plans to prosper me and not to harm me, plans to give me hope and a future. I thank you for your faithfulness in being my source of hope and restoration.

Lord, I surrender my emotional struggles to you. I lay them at your feet, knowing that you can bring healing and renewal to my heart and mind. Help me to trust in your unfailing love and to find comfort in your presence.

Father, in moments of despair and brokenness, remind me of your promise to restore and renew me. Help me to hold onto the truth that you have plans for my well-being and a future filled with hope. Fill me with a deep sense of your hope, knowing that you are working all things together for my good.

Thank you, Lord, for being my hope. I declare that I trust in your plans and rely on your restoration. May your hope continue to strengthen and uplift me, and may your name be glorified in all that I do.

In Jesus' name, I pray.

Amen.

Day 13: "I affirm that God is my healer. He heals the brokenhearted and binds up their wounds." (Psalm 147:3)

Prayer

Heavenly Father,

I come before you today, affirming that you are my healer. Your Word assures me that you heal the brokenhearted and bind up their wounds. I thank you for your faithfulness in being my source of healing and restoration.

Lord, I surrender my brokenness and pain to you. I lay them at your feet, knowing that you are able to bring healing and wholeness to every area of my life. Help me to trust in your unfailing love and to find comfort in your presence.

Father, in moments of emotional turmoil and distress, remind me of your promise to be my healer. Help me to hold onto the truth that you can mend my wounds and bring emotional healing to my heart and mind. Fill me with a deep sense of your healing power, knowing that you can restore and renew me.

Thank you, Lord, for being my healer. I declare that I trust in your healing and rely on your restoration. May your healing continue to bring wholeness to my life, and may your name be glorified in all that I do.

In Jesus' name, I pray.

Amen.

Day 14: "I affirm that God is my comforter. He comforts me in all my afflictions and brings solace to my soul." (2 Corinthians 1:3-4)

Prayer

Heavenly Father,

I come before you today, affirming that you are my comforter. Your Word assures me that you are the God of all comfort, who comforts me in all my afflictions and brings solace to my soul. I thank you for your faithfulness in being my source of comfort and peace.

Lord, I surrender my afflictions and troubles to you. I lay them at your feet, knowing that you are able to bring comfort and solace to my troubled soul. Help me to trust in your unfailing love and to find rest in your presence.

Father, in moments of sadness and distress, remind me of your promise to be my comforter. Help me to hold onto the truth that you are always with me, offering comfort and peace. Fill me with a deep sense of your comforting presence, knowing that I can find solace and tranquility in you.

Thank you, Lord, for being my comforter. I declare that I trust in your comfort and rely on your peace. May your comfort continue to bring healing to my soul, and may your name be glorified in all that I do.

In Jesus' name, I pray.

Amen.

Day 15: "I affirm that God is my refuge. In Him, I find shelter and protection from emotional storms." (Psalm 46:1)

Prayer

Heavenly Father,

I come before you today, affirming that you are my refuge. In you, I find shelter and protection from the emotional storms that surround me. Your Word assures me that you are a strong tower, a place of safety and security. I thank you for your faithfulness in being my source of refuge and strength.

Lord, I surrender my fears and anxieties to you. I lay them at your feet, knowing that you are able to provide refuge and peace in the midst of any storm. Help me to trust in your unfailing love and to find solace in your presence.

Father, in moments of emotional turmoil and distress, remind me of your promise to be my refuge. Help me to hold onto the truth that you are always with me, shielding me from harm. Fill me with a deep sense of your presence, knowing that I can find safety and security in you.

Thank you, Lord, for being my refuge. I declare that I trust in your protection and rely on your comfort. May your refuge continue to be my place of safety, and may your name be glorified in all that I do.

In Jesus' name, I pray.

Amen.

Day 16: "I affirm that God is my strength. He strengthens me in my weakness and gives me the power to overcome emotional challenges." (Philippians 4:13)

Prayer

Heavenly Father,

Heavenly Father,

I come before you today, affirming that you are my strength. Your Word assures me that I can do all things through Christ who strengthens me. I thank you for your faithfulness in being my source of strength and empowerment.

Lord, I surrender my emotional challenges to you. I lay them at your feet, knowing that you can give me the strength to overcome them. Help me to trust in your unfailing love and to find courage in your presence.

Father, in moments of weakness and struggle, remind me of your promise to strengthen me. Help me to hold onto the truth that I can do all things through Christ, who empowers me. Fill me with a deep sense of your strength, knowing that I am not alone in my battles.

Thank you, Lord, for being my strength. I declare that I trust in your power and rely on your guidance.

May your strength continue to empower me to overcome every emotional challenge. May your name be glorified in all that I do.

In Jesus' name, I pray.

Amen.

Day 17: "I affirm that God is my peace. In His presence, I find serenity and calmness, even in the midst of emotional turmoil." (Philippians 4:7)

Prayer

Heavenly Father,

I come before you today, affirming that you are my peace. In your presence, I find serenity and calmness, even in the midst of emotional turmoil. Your Word assures me that your peace surpasses all understanding and can guard my heart and mind. I thank you for your faithfulness in being my source of peace and tranquility.

Lord, I surrender my worries and anxieties to you. I lay them at your feet, knowing that you can bring calm to my troubled soul. Help me to trust in your unfailing love and to find solace in your presence.

Father, in moments of emotional turmoil and distress, remind me of your promise to be my peace. Help me to hold onto the truth that your peace surpasses all understanding and can guard my heart and mind. Fill me with a deep sense of your peace, knowing that I can find rest and tranquility in you.

Thank you, Lord, for being my peace. I declare that I trust in your peace and rely on your presence. May your peace continue to calm my troubled soul, and may your name be glorified in all that I do.

In Jesus' name, I pray.

Amen.

Day 18: "I affirm that God is my hope. In Him, I find the assurance that He will restore and renew my emotional well-being." (Jeremiah 29:11)

Prayer

Dear Heavenly Father,

I come before you today with a heart filled with gratitude and hope. I affirm that you are my hope, my source of strength and restoration. In you, I find the assurance that you will restore and renew my emotional well-being.

Lord, I thank you for your promises, for your word that assures me of your plans for my life. I declare that I trust in your plans, knowing that they are plans to prosper me and not to harm me, plans to give me hope and a future. I surrender my emotions, my hurts, and my brokenness to you, knowing that you are able to heal and restore.

Father, I ask for your healing touch upon my heart. I pray that you will bring healing to the wounds that have caused me pain and brokenness. I ask that you renew my emotional well-being, bringing peace, joy, and wholeness to every area of my life.

Lord, I confess that at times, I have allowed my emotions to control me, to lead me astray. I ask for your forgiveness and for your guidance in managing my emotions in a way that honors you. Help me to surrender my emotions to you, to seek your wisdom and guidance in every situation.

Father, I thank you for your faithfulness. I thank you for your love and compassion that never fails. I know that you are with me in every season of life, and I trust that you will walk with me through this journey of healing and restoration.

In Jesus' name, I pray.

Amen.

Day 19: "I affirm that God is my healer. He heals the brokenhearted and binds up their wounds." (Psalm 147:3)

Prayer

Dear Heavenly Father,

I come before you today with a heart that is in need of healing. I affirm that you are my healer, the one who heals the brokenhearted and binds up their wounds. I declare that I trust in your healing power and believe that you are able to restore and renew my heart.

Lord, I bring before you the brokenness and pain that I carry within me. I ask that you touch those wounded places and bring healing and wholeness. I surrender my hurts, my disappointments, and my sorrows to you, knowing that you are able to bring beauty from ashes.

Father, I thank you for your love and compassion that knows no bounds. I thank you for your faithfulness in walking with me through every season of life. I ask that you would pour out your healing grace upon me, filling me with your peace and joy.

Lord, I confess that, at times, I have tried to find healing in my own strength or in the things of this world. I repent of those times and ask for your forgiveness. Help me to fully rely on you as my healer, knowing that your ways are higher than my ways and your thoughts are higher than my thoughts.

Father, I pray for a deep work of healing in my heart. I ask that you would mend the broken pieces, bringing restoration and wholeness. I pray for healing in my emotions, my thoughts, and my relationships. May your healing touch bring reconciliation and unity where there has been brokenness and division.

Lord, I thank you for the promise of your presence and your healing power. I trust in your timing and your plans for my life. Help me to walk in faith and hope, knowing that you are working all things together for my good.

In Jesus' name, I pray.

Amen.

Day 20: "I affirm that God is my comforter. He comforts me in all my afflictions and brings solace to my soul." (2 Corinthians 1:3-4)

Prayer

Dear Heavenly Father,

I come before you today, acknowledging that you are my comforter. I affirm that in all my afflictions and struggles, you are there to bring solace and comfort to my soul. I declare that I trust in your comforting presence and rely on your strength to carry me through difficult times.

Lord, I thank you for your compassion and love that knows no bounds. I am grateful that you are always near, ready to embrace me in your comforting arms. I surrender my pain, my worries, and my burdens to you, knowing that you are able to bring peace and comfort to my weary soul.

Father, I pray for your comfort to surround me in every situation. When I am overwhelmed by grief, loss, or disappointment, I ask that you wrap me in your loving embrace and bring healing to my wounded heart. When I am burdened by anxiety or fear, I ask that you would calm my troubled mind and fill me with your peace that surpasses all understanding.

Lord, I confess that, at times, I have sought comfort in worldly things or relied on my own strength. I repent of those times and ask for your forgiveness. Help me to turn to you as my ultimate source of comfort, knowing that you are the one who can truly bring healing and restoration to my soul.

Lord, I thank you for your faithfulness in comforting me. I trust in your promises and believe that you will never leave me nor forsake me. Help me to lean on you in times of trouble and to find solace in your loving arms.

In Jesus' name, I pray.

Amen.

Day 21: "I affirm that God is my refuge. In Him, I find shelter and protection from emotional storms." (Psalm 46:1)

Prayer

Dear Heavenly Father,

I come before you today, acknowledging that you are my refuge and shelter. I trust in your unfailing love and seek solace in your presence. Thank you for being my strong tower, a place of safety and security. I surrender my fears, anxieties, and emotional turmoil to you, knowing that you can calm the storms within me. Be my refuge in times of trouble and chaos.

Father, I pray for your peace to fill my heart and mind. When emotions overwhelm me, bring calm and tranquility. Help me find rest in your presence, knowing you are in control and working all things for my good. Forgive me for seeking refuge in worldly things or relying on my own strength. I fully rely on you as my refuge, knowing you bring true peace and protection to my soul.

Thank you for your faithfulness as my refuge. I trust in your promises and believe you guide and protect me. In times of trouble, I run to you and find solace in your loving arms.

In Jesus' name, I pray.

Amen.

Day 22: "I affirm that God is my strength. He strengthens me in my weakness and gives me the power to overcome emotional challenges." (Philippians 4:13)

Prayer

Dear Heavenly Father,

I come before you today, acknowledging that you are my strength. I trust in your power to overcome emotional challenges. Thank you for promising to strengthen me. I surrender my weaknesses, insecurities, and struggles to you, knowing you can give me the strength I need.

Father, fill me with your strength. When emotions overwhelm me, help me lean on you and draw from your limitless strength. Give me the courage to face my emotions and the wisdom to navigate through them with grace and resilience.

Forgive me for relying on my own strength or seeking comfort in worldly things. Help me fully rely on you as my source of strength. Empower me to overcome any emotional challenge.

Thank you for your faithfulness in strengthening me. I trust in your promises and believe you will never leave me. Help me walk in the confidence of your strength, knowing I can do all things through Christ who strengthens me.

In Jesus' name, I pray.

Amen.

Day 23: "I affirm that God is my peace. In His presence, I find serenity and calmness, even in the midst of emotional turmoil." (Philippians 4:7)

Prayer

Dear Heavenly Father,

I come before you today, affirming that you are my peace. I trust in your ability to bring tranquility to my soul, even in the midst of emotional turmoil. Thank you for your promise of peace. I surrender my worries, anxieties, and emotional turmoil to you, knowing that you can bring order and stillness to the chaos within me. Fill me with your peace, guarding my heart and mind in Christ Jesus.

Father, flood my heart and mind with your peace. When emotions threaten to overwhelm me, help me find solace in your presence. Grant me the ability to rest in your peace, knowing you are in control and working all things for my good.

Forgive me for seeking peace in worldly things or relying on my own understanding. Help me fully rely on you as my source of peace. Bring tranquility and calmness to my soul.

Thank you for your faithfulness and for being my peace. I trust in your promises and believe you will never leave me. Help me abide in your peace, walking in the assurance that you are with me, guiding and comforting me.

In Jesus' name, I pray.

Amen.

Day 24: "I affirm that God is my hope. In Him, I find the assurance that He will restore and renew my emotional well-being." (Jeremiah 29:11)

Prayer

Dear Heavenly Father,

I come before you today, affirming that you are my hope. I trust in your plans for my life and believe that you will restore and renew my emotional well-being. Thank you for your promise of hope. I surrender my struggles, hurts, and brokenness to you, knowing that you can bring healing and restoration. Restore my emotional well-being, bringing wholeness and peace to my heart and mind.

Fill me with your hope. When I feel discouraged or overwhelmed, help me turn to you and find strength in your promises. Grant me the ability to hold onto your hope, knowing that you are faithful and have a plan and purpose for my life.

Forgive me for losing sight of your hope and relying on my own understanding. Help me fully trust in you as my source of hope, knowing that you can truly restore and renew my emotional well-being.

Thank you for your faithfulness and for being my hope. I trust in your plans and believe you will never leave me. Help me hold onto your hope, walking in the assurance that you are with me, restoring and renewing my emotional well-being.

In Jesus' name, I pray.

Amen.

Day 25: "I affirm that God is my healer. He heals the brokenhearted and binds up their wounds." (Psalm 147:3)

Prayer

Dear Heavenly Father,

I come before you today, affirming that you are my healer. I trust in your ability to heal the brokenhearted and restore them to wholeness. Thank you for your promise of healing and restoration.

I surrender my emotional wounds, hurts, and brokenness to you. Please bring healing to my heart and mind. Mend the broken pieces within me and restore me to wholeness. I believe that you can heal even the deepest wounds and bring beauty from ashes.

Please touch me with your healing power. When I feel the pain of emotional wounds, help me find comfort in your presence. Grant me the strength to forgive those who have hurt me and release any bitterness or resentment. Fill me with your love and peace, knowing that you can heal and restore all things.

Forgive me for holding onto my pain and allowing it to define me. I repent of those times and ask for your forgiveness. Help me fully trust in you as my healer, knowing that you are the one who can bring true healing and restoration to my heart and mind.

Thank you for your faithfulness as my healer. I trust in your promises and believe that you will never leave me. Help me walk in the assurance of your healing, knowing that you are with me, bringing restoration and wholeness to my life.

In Jesus' name, I pray.

Amen.

Day 26: "I affirm that God is my comforter. He comforts me in all my afflictions and brings solace to my soul." (2 Corinthians 1:3-4)

Prayer

Dear Heavenly Father,

I come before you today, affirming that you are my comforter. I trust in your ability to bring solace to my soul in times of affliction. Please wrap me in your loving arms and fill me with your peace and reassurance. Help me to lean on you and find comfort in your promises. I surrender my burdens to you and ask for your comforting presence to surround me.

Forgive me for seeking comfort in worldly things and relying on my own understanding. I repent of those times and ask for your forgiveness. Help me to fully rely on you as my comforter, knowing that you are the one who can truly bring solace to my soul.

Thank you for your faithfulness as my comforter. I trust in your promises and believe that you will never leave me. Help me to walk in the assurance of your comfort, knowing that you are with me, bringing solace to my soul.

In Jesus' name, I pray.

Amen.

Day 27: "I affirm that God is my refuge. In Him, I find shelter and protection from emotional storms." (Psalm 46:1)

Prayer

Dear Heavenly Father,

I come before you today, affirming that you are my comforter. I trust in your ability to bring solace to my soul in times of affliction. Please wrap me in your loving arms and fill me with your peace and reassurance. Help me to lean on you and find comfort in your promises. I surrender my burdens to you and ask for your comforting presence to surround me.

Forgive me for seeking comfort in worldly things and relying on my own understanding. I repent of those times and ask for your forgiveness. Help me to fully rely on you as my comforter, knowing that you are the one who can truly bring solace to my soul.

Thank you for your faithfulness as my comforter. I trust in your promises and believe that you will never leave me. Help me to walk in the assurance of your comfort, knowing that you are with me, bringing solace to my soul.

In Jesus' name, I pray.

Amen.

Day 28: "I affirm that God is my strength. He strengthens me in my weakness and gives me the power to overcome emotional challenges." (Philippians 4:13)

Prayer

Dear Heavenly Father,

I come before you today, affirming that you are my strength. I trust in your ability to strengthen me and give me the power to overcome emotional challenges. Fill me with your strength and courage, knowing that with you, all things are possible. Help me to rely on your strength rather than my own.

Father, I pray for your strength to be upon me. When I feel weak and overwhelmed, help me to turn to you and find strength in your presence. Grant me the ability to persevere and overcome, knowing that you are with me every step of the way.

Lord, I confess that at times, I have relied on my own strength, only to feel defeated and discouraged. I repent of those times and ask for your forgiveness. Help me to fully trust in you as my strength, knowing that you are the one who can empower me to overcome any challenge.

Thank you for your faithfulness as my strength. I trust in your promises and believe that you will never leave me. Help me to walk in the assurance of your strength, knowing that you are with me, empowering me to overcome any challenge.

In Jesus' name, I pray.

Amen.

Day 29: "I affirm that God is my peace. In His presence, I find serenity and calmness, even in the midst of emotional turmoil." (Philippians 4:7)

Prayer

Dear Heavenly Father,

I come before you today, affirming that you are my peace. Fill me with your peace that surpasses all understanding, especially in times of emotional turmoil. Help me find solace in your presence and trust in your plans for my life. Quiet my anxious thoughts and grant me the ability to rest in your peace, knowing that you are in control.

Father, I pray for your peace to be upon me. When I feel overwhelmed, help me turn to you and find serenity in your presence. Fill me with your calmness and help me trust in your sovereignty. I repent for allowing my emotions to dictate my peace and ask for your forgiveness. Help me fully trust in you as my peace, knowing that you can bring true serenity and calmness to my soul.

Thank you for your faithfulness as my peace. I trust in your promises and believe that you will never leave me. Help me walk in the assurance of your peace, knowing that you are with me, bringing serenity and calmness to my soul.

In Jesus' name, I pray.

Amen.

Day 30: "I affirm that God is my hope. In Him, I find the assurance that He will restore and renew my emotional well-being." (Jeremiah 29:11)

Prayer

Dear Heavenly Father,

I come before you today, affirming that you are my hope. Please restore and renew my emotional well-being. Fill me with hope and assurance, knowing that you have good plans for my life. Help me trust in your timing and find comfort in your promises.

Father, I pray for restoration and renewal. When I feel broken and weary, help me find hope in your presence. Grant me strength and faith to believe that you are working all things together for my good. Help me fully trust in your plans, knowing that you can restore and renew my emotional well-being.

Lord, forgive me for relying on my circumstances for hope instead of relying on you. Help me trust in you as my hope, knowing that you can bring restoration and renewal to my emotional well-being.

Thank you for your faithfulness as my hope. I trust in your promises and believe that you will never leave me. Help me walk in the assurance of your hope, knowing that you are with me, bringing restoration and renewal to my emotional well-being.

In Jesus' name, I pray.

Amen.

I AM WHO HE SAYS I AM

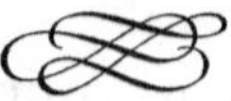

Day 1: "I affirm that I am fearfully and wonderfully made by God. I am created in His image and have inherent worth and value." (Psalm 139:14)

Prayer

Dear Heavenly Father,

I come before you today, affirming that I am fearfully and wonderfully made by you. Thank you for creating me in your image and giving me inherent worth and value. Help me fully embrace this truth and see myself as you see me, with love and acceptance.

Heal any wounds or hurts that have caused me to doubt my worth and value. Restore my confidence and self-esteem, knowing that I am fearfully and wonderfully made by you. Help me walk in the truth of who I am in you.

Forgive me for allowing the opinions of others or society to define my worth and value. Help me to find my identity in you alone and not in the opinions of others.

Thank you for your faithfulness in creating me fearfully and wonderfully. I trust in your promises and believe that you will never leave me. Help me walk in the assurance of my worth and value in you, knowing that I am loved and cherished by you.

In Jesus' name, I pray.

Amen.

Day 2: "I affirm that I am loved unconditionally by God. His love for me is not based on my performance or appearance, but on His grace and mercy." (Romans 5:8)

Prayer

Dear Heavenly Father,

I come before you today, affirming that I am loved unconditionally by you. Thank you for your grace and mercy. Help me embrace the truth that your love for me is not based on my performance or appearance. Fill me with a deep understanding of your love and help me rest in its assurance. Heal any wounds that have caused me to doubt your love.

Restore my confidence and security in your unwavering and unchanging love. Forgive me for seeking worthiness in my performance or appearance. Help me fully embrace the truth that your love for me is unconditional and cannot be earned. May I find my security and identity in your love alone.

Thank you for your faithfulness in loving me unconditionally. I trust in your promises and believe that you will never leave me. Help me walk in the assurance of your love, knowing that I am deeply loved by you.

In Jesus' name, I pray.

Amen.

Day 3: "I affirm that I am chosen by God. He has called me His own and has a purpose and plan for my life." (1 Peter 2:9)

Prayer

Dear Heavenly Father,

Thank you for choosing me and giving me a purpose and plan for my life. Help me embrace the truth that I am chosen by you and see myself as a beloved child of God. Guide me in fulfilling your calling and give me the strength to trust in your provision and guidance.

Forgive me for allowing the opinions of others or my own insecurities to overshadow your calling on my life. Help me fully embrace the truth that I am chosen by you and that your calling is greater than any human opinion or limitation.

Thank you for choosing me and calling me your own. I trust in your promises and believe that you will never leave me. Help me walk in the assurance of being chosen by you, knowing that I am loved and cherished by you.

In Jesus' name, I pray.

Amen.

Day 4: "I affirm that I am forgiven by God. He has washed away my sins and remembers them no more." (Psalm 103:12)

Prayer

Dear Heavenly Father,

Thank you for forgiving me and washing away my sins. Help me embrace the truth that I am forgiven by you. Fill me with a deep understanding of your forgiveness and help me let go of guilt and shame. Restore my confidence in your forgiveness and help me walk in the freedom it brings.

Heal any wounds that have caused me to doubt your forgiveness. Help me to fully embrace the truth that my past does not define my future. Guide me in finding my identity in your forgiveness and walking in the freedom it brings.

Thank you for your faithfulness in forgiving me. I trust in your promises and believe that you will never hold my sins against me. Help me walk in the assurance of your forgiveness, knowing that I am loved and accepted by you.

In Jesus' name, I pray.

Amen.

Day 5: "I affirm that I am a child of God. I am adopted into His family and have the privilege of calling Him my Father." (John 1:12)

Prayer

Dear Heavenly Father,

Thank you for adopting me into your family and making me your child. Help me fully embrace the truth that I am a child of God. Fill me with a deep understanding of my worth and value as your beloved child. Guide me in living out my identity as your child and bring glory to your name.

Forgive me for allowing the opinions of others or my own insecurities to overshadow my identity as your child. Help me to fully embrace the truth that my identity is found in you alone.

Thank you for adopting me into your family. I trust in your promises and believe that you will never leave me. Help me walk in the assurance of being your child, knowing that I am loved and cherished by you.

In Jesus' name, I pray.

Amen.

Day 6: "I affirm that I am accepted by God. He accepts me just as I am, with all my flaws and imperfections." (Romans 15:7)

Prayer

Dear Heavenly Father,

Thank you for accepting me just as I am. Help me embrace the truth that I am fully accepted by you. Fill me with a deep understanding of your love and acceptance, and help me rest in its assurance.

Heal any wounds or hurts that have caused me to doubt my acceptance by you. Restore my confidence and security in your acceptance, knowing that it is not based on anything I do or don't do. Help me walk in the truth of your acceptance for me.

Forgive me for seeking acceptance from others or trying to earn your acceptance through my own efforts. Help me fully embrace the truth that I am accepted by you and that your acceptance is all I need. May I find my security and identity in your acceptance alone.

Thank you for faithfully accepting me. I trust in your promises and believe that you will never reject me. Help me walk in the assurance of your acceptance, knowing that I am loved and cherished by you.

In Jesus' name, I pray.

Amen.

Day 7: "I affirm that I am valuable to God. He gave His Son, Jesus, to die for me, showing the immeasurable value He places on my life." (Matthew 10:31)

Prayer

Dear Heavenly Father,

Thank you for valuing me and giving your Son, Jesus, for my life. Help me fully embrace the truth that I am valuable to you. Restore my confidence in your love, and help me see myself as your precious child.

Heal any wounds that have caused me to doubt my value. Help me let go of others' opinions and my own self-doubt. Guide me in finding my identity and worth in your love alone.

Thank you for your immeasurable love and the value you place on my life. I trust in your promises and believe that I am cherished by you. Help me walk in the assurance of my value to you, knowing that I am loved beyond measure.

In Jesus' name, I pray.

Amen.

Day 8: "I affirm that I am equipped by God. He has given me unique gifts and talents to fulfill His purposes." (Ephesians 2:10)

Prayer

Dear Heavenly Father,

Thank you for equipping me with unique gifts and talents. Help me embrace the truth that I am equipped by you. Guide me in using my abilities for your glory, and give me the wisdom and courage to step out in faith.

Forgive me for doubting my abilities and comparing myself to others. Help me fully embrace the truth that I am uniquely equipped by you and that my worth is not determined by comparison. May I find my identity and purpose in you alone.

Thank you for equipping me and using me for your glory. I trust in your promises and believe that I am loved and empowered by you.

In Jesus' name, I pray.

Amen.

Day 9: "I affirm that I am strong in God. He gives me the strength to overcome challenges and persevere in difficult times." (Philippians 4:13)

Prayer

Dear Heavenly Father,

Thank you for the strength you give me to overcome challenges and persevere in difficult times. Help me fully embrace the truth that I am strong in you. Fill me with a deep understanding of the strength you provide, and help me rely on you in all circumstances.

Give me the perseverance to keep going, even when things seem impossible. Help me trust in your power and lean on you for strength. I repent of allowing fear and doubt to overshadow my strength in you. Help me embrace the truth that I am strong in you, finding my identity and confidence in your strength alone.

Thank you for empowering me to overcome challenges. I trust in your promises and believe that I am strong in you. Help me walk in the assurance of my strength, knowing that I am loved and empowered by you.

In Jesus' name, I pray.

Amen.

Day 10: "I affirm that I am a new creation in Christ. The old has passed away, and I am made new in Him." (2 Corinthians 5:17)

Prayer

Dear Heavenly Father,

Thank you for making me a new creation in Christ. Help me fully embrace this truth and understand the newness and freshness that comes from being in Him.

Guide me in living out my new identity and letting go of old habits and patterns that no longer align with who I am in Christ. Empower me to reflect your love and grace in all that I do.

Forgive me for allowing my past mistakes and failures to define me. Help me embrace the truth that I am a new creation in Christ, finding my worth and identity in Him alone.

Thank you for the transformative power of your love and grace. I trust in your promises and believe that I am a new creation in Christ. Help me walk in the assurance of my new identity, knowing that I am loved and redeemed by you.

In Jesus' name, I pray.

Amen.

Day 11: "I affirm that I am blessed by God. He has showered me with His blessings and favor." (Ephesians 1:3)

Prayer

Heavenly Father,

Thank you for blessing me and showing me a favor. Help me fully embrace the truth that I am blessed by you. Give me a deep understanding of your abundant blessings.

Please continue to bless and favor me in my life. Help me recognize and appreciate the ways you are working. Open my eyes to see the blessings you have already given me and fill me with gratitude.

Forgive me for allowing circumstances or comparison to overshadow your blessings. Help me fully embrace the truth that I am blessed by you alone. Guide me in finding my worth and identity in your love and favor.

Thank you for showering me with blessings and favor. I trust in your promises and believe that I am blessed by you. Help me walk in the assurance of your blessings, knowing that I am loved and favored by you.

In Jesus' name, I pray.

Amen.

Day 12: "I affirm that I am valuable to God. He knows the number of hairs on my head and cares for every detail of my life." (Matthew 10:30)

Prayer

Heavenly Father,

Thank you for affirming my values and caring for every detail of my life. Help me fully embrace the truth that I am valuable to you. Fill me with a deep understanding of my worth and significance in your sight.

Guide me and give me strength as I navigate through life. Help me remember that I am valuable to you and that you are intimately involved in every aspect of my life. Give me the confidence to trust in your plans and purposes for me.

Forgive me for allowing the opinions of others or my own self-doubt to diminish my sense of value. Help me fully embrace the truth that I am valuable to you and that my worth is not determined by others. May I find my identity and value in your love and care.

Thank you for affirming my values and caring for every detail of my life. I trust in your promises and believe that I am valuable to you. Help me walk in the assurance of my worth, knowing that I am loved and cherished by you.

In Jesus' name, I pray.

Amen.

Day 13: "I affirm that I am loved by God with an everlasting love. His love for me is constant and unwavering." (Jeremiah 31:3)

Prayer

Heavenly Father,

Thank you for loving me with an everlasting love. Help me fully embrace this truth and understand the depth and constancy of your love.

Surround me with your love and help me to experience it in tangible ways. Fill me with a deep understanding of your love and enable me to share it with others.

Forgive me for allowing circumstances or the opinions of others to overshadow your love for me. Help me to fully embrace the truth that I am loved by you with everlasting love, finding my worth and identity in your love alone.

Thank you for loving me with an everlasting love. I trust in your promises and believe that I am loved by you. Help me walk in the assurance of your love, knowing that I am cherished and valued by you.

In Jesus' name, I pray.

Amen.

Day 14: "I affirm that I am created for a purpose. God has a unique plan for my life and will guide me in fulfilling it." (Jeremiah 29:11)

Prayer

Heavenly Father,

Thank you for creating me for a purpose and guiding me in fulfilling it. Help me fully embrace this truth and understand the unique plan you have for my life.

Guide me and give me strength as I seek to fulfill my purpose. Help me discern your will and walk in obedience to your leading. Give me the courage and strength to pursue the calling you have placed on my life.

Forgive me for allowing fear or comparison to hinder me from embracing my purpose. Help me fully embrace the truth that I am created for a purpose, finding my worth and identity in fulfilling your plan for my life.

Thank you for creating me for a purpose and guiding me in fulfilling it. I trust in your promises and believe that I am created for a purpose. Help me walk in the assurance of my purpose, knowing that I am loved and empowered by you.

In Jesus' name, I pray.

Amen.

Day 15: "I affirm that I am a temple of the Holy Spirit. God's Spirit dwells within me, empowering and guiding me." (1 Corinthians 6:19)

Prayer

Heavenly Father,

Thank you for making me a temple of the Holy Spirit. Help me fully embrace this truth and understand the power and guidance that comes from your Spirit.

Empower me, Holy Spirit, and guide me in every decision and action. Help me yield to your leading and walk in obedience to your will. May I bring glory to your name through my life.

Forgive me for neglecting to acknowledge your presence and power within me. Help me fully embrace the truth that I am a temple of the Holy Spirit and live in the fullness of your empowerment and guidance.

Thank you for making me a temple of the Holy Spirit and for empowering and guiding me. I trust in your promises and believe that your Spirit dwells within me. Help me walk in the assurance of your Spirit's presence, knowing that I am loved and empowered by you.

In Jesus' name, I pray.

Amen.

Day 16: "I affirm that I am an overcomer. Through Christ, I have victory over every obstacle and challenge." (Romans 8:37)

Prayer

Heavenly Father,

Thank you for making me an overcomer through Christ. Help me fully embrace this truth and understand the power and victory that comes from Him.

Give me strength and guidance as I face obstacles and challenges. Help me rely on your power and trust in your promises. Give me the courage and perseverance to overcome every obstacle.

Forgive me for allowing fear or discouragement to hinder me from embracing my identity as an overcomer. Help me fully embrace the truth that I am an overcomer through Christ, finding my strength and victory in Him alone.

Thank you for making me an overcomer through Christ and giving me victory over every obstacle. I trust in your promises and believe that I can overcome through Him. Help me walk in the assurance of my identity as an overcomer, knowing that I am loved and empowered by you.

In Jesus' name, I pray.

Amen.

Day 17: "I affirm that I am a light in the world. God has called me to shine His love and truth to those around me." (Matthew 5:14)

Prayer

Heavenly Father,

Thank you for calling me to be a light in the world. Help me fully embrace this truth and understand the impact I can make through your love and truth.

Guide and empower me as I seek to shine your light. Help me reflect your love and truth in all that I do. Give me the courage to share your message with those around me.

Forgive me for allowing fear or doubt to hinder me from embracing my role as a light. Help me fully embrace the truth that I am a light in the world, finding my purpose and identity in shining your love and truth.

Thank you for calling me to be a light in the world and empowering me to shine your love and truth. I trust in your promises and believe that I can make a difference through your light. Help me walk in the assurance of my role as a light, knowing that I am loved and empowered by you.

In Jesus' name, I pray.

Amen.

Day 18: "I affirm that I am a vessel of God's grace. His grace is sufficient for me, and His power is made perfect in my weakness." (2 Corinthians 12:9)

Prayer

Heavenly Father,

Thank you for making me a vessel of your grace. Help me embrace the truth that your grace is sufficient for me, and your power is made perfect in my weakness.

Fill me with a deep understanding of the power and sufficiency of your grace. Use me to bring healing and restoration to those who are hurting.

Forgive me for doubting my worthiness to be a vessel of your grace. Help me fully embrace the truth that I am chosen and loved by you. Help me let go of doubt and insecurity and embrace the power and sufficiency of your grace.

Thank you for choosing me to be a vessel of your grace and for empowering me to make a difference in the lives of others. I trust in your promises and believe that your grace is sufficient for me. Help me walk in the assurance of my role as a vessel of your grace, knowing that I am loved and empowered by you.

In Jesus' name, I pray.

Amen.

Day 19: "I affirm that I am a beloved child of God. He delights in me and rejoices over me with singing." (Zephaniah 3:17)

Prayer

Heavenly Father,

Thank you for loving me and delighting in me as your child. Help me fully embrace the truth that I am loved and cherished by you. Fill me with a deep understanding of your delight in me.

Guide me in walking in the confidence of my identity as your beloved child. Help me let go of doubt and insecurity and embrace the joy and confidence that comes from being your child.

Thank you for loving me and delighting in me as your child. I trust in your promises and believe that I am cherished by you. Help me to walk in the assurance of my identity as your beloved child, knowing that I am loved and empowered by you.

In Jesus' name, I pray.

Amen.

Day 20: "I affirm that I am a conqueror. In all things, I am more than a conqueror through Christ who loves me." (Romans 8:37)

Prayer

Heavenly Father,

Thank you for making me a conqueror through Christ's love. Help me embrace this truth and trust in your strength.

Guide and empower me as I face challenges and obstacles. Give me the courage and perseverance to overcome every trial.

Forgive me for allowing fear or discouragement to hinder me from fully embracing my identity as a conqueror. Help me let go of doubt and fully embrace the truth that I am more than a conqueror through Christ's love.

I also pray for those struggling to believe in their ability to conquer. Lift them up and fill them with the truth that they are more than conquerors through Christ. Help them let go of fear and discouragement, and embrace the power and victory that comes from Him.

Thank you for making me a conqueror through Christ and giving me victory over every obstacle. I trust in your promises and believe that I am more than a conqueror through Him. Help me walk in the assurance of my identity as a conqueror, knowing that I am loved and empowered by you.

In Jesus' name, I pray.

Amen.

Day 21: "I affirm that I am a work in progress. God is continually shaping and molding me into His image." (Philippians 1:6)

Prayer

Heavenly Father,

Thank you for continually shaping and molding me into your image. Help me embrace the truth that I am a work in progress.

Guide me and give me wisdom as I grow and transform. Help me surrender to your will and trust in your plan for my life. Give me patience and perseverance during this process.

Forgive me for doubting my journey of growth and transformation. Help me fully embrace the truth that you are at work in me and will bring the good work to completion.

Thank you for your faithfulness in shaping and molding me. I trust in your promises and believe that you will complete the good work in me. Help me walk in the assurance of my identity as a work in progress, knowing that I am loved and empowered by you.

In Jesus' name, I pray.

Amen.

Day 22: "I affirm that I am a vessel of God's love. His love flows through me, touching the lives of those around me."

(1 John 4:7)

Prayer

Heavenly Father,

Thank you for making me a vessel of your love. Help me fully embrace this truth and trust in your power.

Guide me to show compassion, kindness, and forgiveness to others, reflecting your love in all that I do.

Forgive me for allowing fear or self-doubt to hinder me from fully embracing my role as a vessel of your love. Help me to let go of those doubts and fully embrace the truth that your love flows through me, touching the lives of those around me.

Thank you for choosing me to be a vessel of your love and for empowering me to make a difference in the lives of others. I trust in your promises and believe that your love can flow through me, touching the lives of those around me. Help me walk in the assurance of my role as a vessel of your love, knowing that I am loved and empowered by you.

In Jesus' name, I pray.

Amen.

Day 23: "I affirm that I am a chosen instrument of God. He has appointed me to bear fruit that will last." (John

15:16)

Prayer

Heavenly Father,

Thank you for choosing me as your instrument. Help me embrace this truth and trust in your purpose for my life.

Guide and empower me as I fulfill my calling. Give me wisdom and courage to bear fruit that brings glory to your name.

Forgive me for allowing self-doubt or fear to hinder me from fully embracing my identity as your chosen instrument. Help me let go of those doubts and fully embrace the truth that you have appointed me for a specific purpose.

Thank you for choosing me and appointing me to bear fruit that will last. I trust in your promises and believe that you will empower me to fulfill my calling. Help me walk in the assurance of my identity as your chosen instrument, knowing that I am loved and empowered by you.

In Jesus' name, I pray.

Amen.

Day 24: "I affirm that I am a child of light. I walk in the light of God's truth and reflect His glory." (Ephesians 5:8)

Prayer

Heavenly Father,

Thank you for making me a child of light. Help me embrace this truth and walk in your light.

Guide me to reflect on your glory and live a life that pleases you.

Forgive me for allowing darkness or self-doubt to hinder me from fully embracing my identity as your child of light. Help me let go of those doubts and fully embrace the truth that your light shines through me.

Thank you for making me a child of light and empowering me to reflect on your glory. I trust in your promises and believe that your light shines through me. Help me walk in the assurance of my identity as your child of light, knowing that I am loved and empowered by you.

In Jesus' name, I pray.

Amen.

Day 25: "I affirm that I am a co-heir with Christ. I share in His inheritance and have access to all the blessings of God." (Romans 8:17)

Prayer

Heavenly Father,

Thank you for making me a co-heir with Christ. Help me fully embrace this truth and trust in the blessings and inheritance that come from being in Him.

Guide and empower me as I walk in my identity as a co-heir with Christ. Give me the wisdom and courage to live a life that reflects His blessings and abundance.

Forgive me for allowing self-doubt or fear to hinder me from fully embracing my identity as a co-heir with Christ. Help me let go of those doubts and fully embrace the truth that I share in His inheritance and have access to all the blessings of God.

Thank you for making me a co-heir with Christ and granting me access to all the blessings of God. I trust in your promises and believe that I am united with Him. Help me walk in the assurance of my identity as a co-heir with Christ, knowing that I am loved and empowered by you.

In Jesus' name, I pray.

Amen.

Day 26: "I affirm that I am a living testimony of God's grace. His grace has transformed my life and continues to work in me." (Ephesians 2:8-9)

Prayer

Heavenly Father,

Thank you for your transforming grace in my life. Help me fully embrace this truth and trust in its power.

Guide me to reflect your grace to others and live a life that brings honor to your name.

Forgive me for doubting my testimony of your grace. Help me let go of those doubts and fully embrace the truth that your grace has transformed my life.

Thank you for your transforming grace. I trust in your promises and believe that your grace is at work in me. Help me walk in the assurance of my testimony, knowing that I am loved and empowered by you.

In Jesus' name, I pray.

Amen.

Day 27: "I affirm that I am a vessel of God's peace. His peace guards my heart and mind, even in the midst of challenges." (Philippians 4:7)

Prayer

Heavenly Father,

Thank you for making me a vessel of your peace. Help me fully embrace this truth and trust in the power of your peace.

Guide me to be a source of peace to others, especially in challenging times. Help me reflect on your peace and bring comfort and healing to those around me.

Forgive me for allowing worry or anxiety to hinder me from embracing my role as a vessel of your peace. Help me let go of those doubts and fully embrace the truth that your peace guards my heart and mind.

Thank you for making me a vessel of your peace and guarding my heart and mind with your peace. I trust in your promises and believe that your peace flows through me. Help me walk in the assurance of my role as a vessel of your peace, knowing that I am loved and empowered by you.

In Jesus' name, I pray.

Amen.

Day 28: "I affirm that I am a disciple of Christ. I follow Him and seek to live according to His teachings." (John 8:31)

Prayer

Heavenly Father,

I affirm that I am a disciple of Christ, choosing to follow Him and live according to His teachings. Thank you for the truth of John 8:31, that as I continue in His word, I am truly His disciple.

Help me fully embrace my identity as a disciple of Christ and understand its significance. Guide me, empower me, and give me the wisdom to live a life that reflects His teachings and brings glory to your name.

Forgive me for allowing distractions and temptations to hinder me from fully embracing my identity as a disciple. Help me let go of those hindrances and fully embrace the truth that I am called to follow Him and live according to His teachings.

Thank you for calling me to be a disciple of Christ and for empowering me through your Spirit. Help me walk in the assurance of my identity as a disciple, knowing that I am loved and guided by you.

In Jesus' name, I pray.

Amen.

Day 29: "I affirm that I am a citizen of heaven. My true home is with God, and I eagerly await the day when I will be with Him forever." (Philippians 3:20)

Prayer

Heavenly Father,

Thank you for making me a citizen of heaven. Help me fully embrace this truth and understand its significance.

Guide me to reflect the values and principles of your kingdom in all that I do. Give me a heart that longs for your presence and a desire to bring your kingdom to earth.

Forgive me for allowing the distractions and temptations of this world to hinder me from fully embracing my identity as a citizen of heaven. Help me let go of those hindrances and fully embrace the truth that my true home is with you.

Thank you for calling me to be a citizen of heaven and for the promise of eternal life with you. I trust in your promises and eagerly await the day when I will be with you forever. Help me walk in the assurance of my identity as a citizen of heaven, knowing that I am loved and destined for eternity with you.

In Jesus' name, I pray.

Amen.

Day 30: "I affirm that I am a witness of God's love and truth. I share the good news of Jesus Christ with others, pointing them to Him." (Acts 1:8)

Prayer

Heavenly Father,

I affirm that I am a witness of your love and truth. Thank you for empowering me through your Spirit to share the good news of Jesus Christ with others.

Help me fully embrace my role as a witness and understand its significance. Guide me, empower me, and give me boldness and clarity as I share your love and truth with those around me.

Forgive me for allowing fear or doubt to hinder me from fully embracing my role as a witness. Help me let go of those hindrances and fully embrace the truth that I am called to share your love and truth.

Thank you for calling me to be a witness of your love and truth. I trust in your promises and believe that I am empowered by your Spirit. Help me walk in the assurance of my role as a witness, knowing that I am loved and guided by you.

In Jesus' name, I pray.

Amen.

Day 31: "I affirm that I am fearfully and wonderfully made by God. I am created in His image and have inherent worth and value." (Psalm 139:14)

Prayer

Heavenly Father,

Thank you for creating me fearfully and wonderfully. Help me embrace the truth that I am made in your image and have inherent worth and value.

Guide me to see myself and others through your eyes with love and compassion. Give me the strength to overcome negative self-image and comparison and to embrace the unique person you created me to be.

Forgive me for allowing the opinions of others or the pressures of this world to hinder my identity and worth. Help me let go of negative thoughts and influences and fully embrace the truth that I am fearfully and wonderfully made by you.

Thank you for creating me fearfully and wonderfully and for giving me worth and value. I trust in your promises and believe that I am loved and cherished by you. Help me walk in the assurance of my identity and worth, knowing that I am fearfully and wonderfully made by you.

In Jesus' name, I pray.

Amen.

THE BROKEN HOME

Day 1: "I affirm that God loves me unconditionally, even in a divorce or single-parent home. He is always with me and will never leave me." (Deuteronomy 31:6)

Prayer

Heavenly Father,

Thank you for your unconditional love and constant presence in my life, even in difficult circumstances like divorce or being in a single-parent home. Help me fully embrace the truth that you love me and are always with me, no matter what I'm going through. Give me strength and comfort as I navigate these challenges, and guide me to make decisions that honor you and bring peace to my life.

Forgive me for doubting your love and presence at times. Help me let go of those doubts and fully embrace the truth that you are always with me, even in difficult times.

Thank you for your unwavering love and constant presence in my life. I trust in your promises and believe that you will never leave me. Help me walk in the assurance of your love and presence, knowing that I am cherished and cared for by you.

In Jesus' name, I pray.

Amen.

Day 2: "I declare that God is my Father and He will take care of me. He knows my needs and will provide for me." (Matthew 6:26)

Prayer

Heavenly Father,

Thank you for being my Father and for taking care of me. I trust in your promises and believe that you will provide for all my needs. Help me fully embrace the truth that you are my Father and that you will take care of me. Fill me with a deep understanding of the significance of your provision and care.

Guide me to trust in your faithfulness and to rely on you for all that I need. Give me the wisdom to seek your kingdom first and to trust that you will provide everything else.

Forgive me for allowing worry and doubt to hinder me from fully embracing your provision and care. Help me let go of any worries or anxieties and fully embrace the truth that you are my Father and that you will take care of me.

Thank you for being my Father and for taking care of me. I trust in your promises and believe that you will provide for all my needs. Help me walk in the assurance of your provision and care, knowing that I am loved and cared for by you.

In Jesus' name, I pray.

Amen.

Day 3: "I affirm that I am not alone. God is my constant companion, and He will comfort me in times of sadness or loneliness." (Psalm 34:18)

Prayer

Heavenly Father,

Thank you for being my constant companion and comforting me in times of sadness or loneliness. Help me embrace the truth that you are always with me and that you are my source of comfort and strength. Fill me with the understanding of your presence in my life.

Father, I surrender any feelings of sadness or loneliness to you. Help me find solace in your presence and lean on you for strength. Give me the assurance that you are near and will never leave me.

Forgive me for forgetting your constant companionship and allowing sadness or loneliness to consume me. Help me fully embrace the truth that you are always with me and let go of these negative feelings.

Thank you for being my constant companion and comforting me. I trust in your promises and believe that I am never alone. Help me walk in the assurance of your presence, knowing that you are always with me.

In Jesus' name, I pray.

Amen.

Day 4: "I declare that God is my refuge and strength. He is my safe place, and I can run to Him for comfort and peace." (Psalm 46:1)

Prayer

Heavenly Father,

Thank you for being my refuge and strength. Help me to fully embrace the truth that I can find safety and peace in your presence. Fill me with the understanding of seeking refuge in you.

I surrender any fears or anxieties that I may be carrying. Give me comfort and peace in times of trouble or distress. Help me to find solace in your presence and to lean on you for strength.

Forgive me for allowing fear and worry to consume me. Help me let go of any fears or anxieties and fully embrace the truth that you are my safe place.

Thank you for being my refuge and strength. I trust in your promises and believe that I can find safety and peace in your presence. Help me walk in the assurance of your refuge and strength, knowing that I am secure and protected by you.

In Jesus' name, I pray.

Amen.

Day 5: "I affirm that God is my healer. He can heal my heart and bring restoration to my family." (Psalm 147:3)

Prayer

Heavenly Father,

Thank you for being my healer and for bringing restoration to my family. I surrender any pain or brokenness to you and fully embrace the truth that you have the power to heal and restore. Bring healing to my heart and my family, and restore relationships. Help me to trust in your healing touch and let go of any doubts or disbelief.

Thank you for your faithfulness and for working in our lives. I trust in your promises and believe that you can bring healing and restoration. Help me to walk in the assurance of your healing touch, knowing that you are at work in my life.

In Jesus' name, I pray.

Amen.

Day 6: "I declare that God is my provider. He will meet all my needs according to His riches in glory." (Philippians 4:19)

Prayer

Heavenly Father,

Thank you for being my provider. I surrender my worries and anxieties about my needs to you. Help me to fully embrace the truth that you have abundant resources to meet all my needs. Provide for me in every area of my life, and give me the assurance that you are faithful to provide.

Forgive me for doubting your ability to provide for me. Help me let go of worries and anxieties and fully trust in your provision.

Thank you for being my provider and for meeting all my needs. I trust in your promises and believe that you will provide for all that I need. Help me walk in the assurance of your provision, knowing that I am loved and cared for by you.

In Jesus' name, I pray.

Amen.

Day 7: "I affirm that God is my helper. He will give me strength and wisdom to navigate through any challenges I may face." (Psalm 121:2)

Prayer

Dear Heavenly Father,

I come before you today with a humble heart, acknowledging that you are my helper. I affirm and declare that you are the source of my strength and wisdom, and I trust in your unfailing guidance as I face the challenges that lie ahead.

Lord, I thank you for your promise in Psalm 121:2 that you will give me the strength and wisdom to navigate through any obstacles that come my way. I am grateful for your unwavering presence in my life, knowing that I am never alone in my struggles.

In times of uncertainty, I ask for your divine intervention. Grant me the clarity of mind to make wise decisions and the discernment to choose the right path. Fill me with your peace that surpasses all understanding so that I may remain steadfast in the face of adversity.

Father, I surrender my fears and anxieties to you, knowing that you are in control. Help me to trust in your perfect plan for my life, even when the road ahead seems daunting. Strengthen my faith that I may rely on your promises and find comfort in your unfailing love.

I pray for your divine favor and blessings to be upon me as I navigate through the challenges that lie ahead. May your wisdom guide my steps, and may your strength sustain me in every situation. I believe that with you by my side, I can overcome any obstacle that comes my way.

Thank you, Lord, for being my helper. I place my trust in you, knowing that you will never leave me nor forsake me. In Jesus' name, I pray.

Amen.

Day 8: "I declare that God is my peace. He will calm my fears and anxieties and give me a sense of security." (John 14:27)

Prayer

Dear Heavenly Father,

I come before you today, declaring that you are my peace. I thank you for the promise in John 14:27 that you will calm my fears and anxieties and give me a sense of security. I trust in your unfailing love and faithfulness to fulfill this promise in my life.

Lord, I surrender my fears and anxieties to you. I lay them at your feet, knowing that you are the source of true peace. I ask that you calm the storms within me and replace my worries with your perfect peace. Help me to cast all my cares upon you, for I know that you care for me.

In moments of uncertainty and doubt, remind me of your presence. Fill me with your peace that surpasses all understanding so that I may rest in your loving embrace. Help me to trust in your plan for my life, knowing that you are in control and that you have good things in store for me.

Father, I ask for your guidance and wisdom as I navigate through the challenges and uncertainties of life. Give me the discernment to make wise decisions and the courage to step out in faith. Help me to rely on your strength and not on my own understanding.

I declare that you are my peace, and I choose to fix my eyes on you. I will not be overcome by fear or anxiety, for you are with me. Thank you for your constant presence and for the peace that you provide. May your peace guard my heart and mind in Christ Jesus.

In Jesus' name, I pray.

Amen.

Day 9: "I affirm that God is my joy. He will fill my heart with His joy, even in difficult times." (Psalm 16:11)

Prayer

Dear Heavenly Father,

I come before you today, affirming that you are my joy. I thank you for the promise in Psalm 16:11 that you will fill my heart with your joy, even in difficult times. I declare that my joy is not dependent on my circumstances but on your presence and love.

Lord, I surrender my worries and anxieties to you. I choose to focus on your goodness and faithfulness, knowing that you are in control of every situation. I ask that you fill my heart with your joy so that it may overflow and bring light to those around me.

In moments of sadness or despair, remind me of your joy. Help me to find comfort and strength in your presence. I trust that you will turn my mourning into dancing and replace my sorrow with your joy.

Father, I ask for your joy to be my strength. Help me to rejoice in you always, even when faced with trials and challenges. Teach me to find joy in the little things and to be grateful for your blessings.

I declare that your joy is my strength, and I choose to embrace it. I will not let circumstances steal my joy, for you are with me. Thank you for the joy that you provide, and may it shine through me as a testimony of your love and faithfulness.

In Jesus' name, I pray.

Amen.

Day 10: "I declare that God is my guide. He will lead me on the right path and show me His perfect plan for my life." (Psalm 32:8)

Prayer

Dear Heavenly Father,

I come before you today, declaring that you are my guide. I thank you for the promise in Psalm 32:8 that you will lead me on the right path and show me your perfect plan for my life. I trust in your wisdom and guidance as I navigate through the decisions and challenges that lie ahead.

Lord, I surrender my own plans and desires to you. I acknowledge that your ways are higher than my ways, and your thoughts are higher than my thoughts. Help me to align my will with yours and to seek your guidance in all that I do.

I ask for your divine direction and clarity of mind. Open my eyes to see the path that you have set before me and give me the courage to walk in it. Guide my steps and order my every decision according to your perfect will.

Father, I trust that you have a purpose and a plan for my life. I believe that you will lead me on the right path and equip me with everything I need to fulfill your calling. Help me trust in your timing and be patient as you work out your plan in my life.

I declare that you are my guide, and I choose to follow your lead. I surrender my own understanding and lean on your wisdom.

Thank you for your faithfulness and for the assurance that you will never leave me nor forsake me.

In Jesus' name, I pray.

Amen.

Day 11: "I affirm that God is my strength. He will give me the strength to overcome any challenges or obstacles I may face." (Isaiah 40:29)

Prayer

Heavenly Father,

I acknowledge that you are my strength, as stated in Isaiah 40:29. I surrender the brokenness in my home to you, asking for healing and restoration. Fill me with an understanding of your strength and its significance in my family.

Grant me the strength to persevere through difficult times and seek reconciliation and healing. Help me to love and forgive, even when it feels impossible. Empower me to be a source of peace and unity within my family. Guide and support me, assuring me of your presence.

Forgive me for relying on my own strength and wisdom to fix the brokenness in my home. I fully embrace the truth that you are my strength and release any self-reliance or doubt. Teach me to lean on you and trust in your power to bring healing and restoration.

Thank you for being my strength and empowering me to overcome. I trust in your promises and believe that you can bring healing and restoration to my broken home. Help me walk in the assurance of your strength, knowing that you are at work in my family.

In Jesus' name, I pray.

Amen.

Day 12: "I declare that God is my comforter. He will bring me comfort and peace in times of sadness or grief." (2 Corinthians 1:3-4)

Prayer

Heavenly Father,

Thank you for being my comforter in times of sadness or grief. I surrender the brokenness in my home to you, asking for healing and peace. Fill my family with the understanding of your comfort and its significance.

Bring comfort to each member of my family who is hurting or grieving. Wrap your loving arms around us and heal our hearts. Assure us of your presence and guide us towards peace.

Forgive me for seeking comfort in worldly things or relying on my own strength. I fully embrace the truth that you are my comforter and release any reliance on temporary sources of solace.

Thank you for being my comforter and bringing healing and peace to my broken home. I trust in your promises and believe that you can bring comfort in times of sadness or grief. Help me walk in the assurance of your comfort, knowing that you are at work in my family.

In Jesus' name, I pray.

Amen.

Day 13: "I affirm that God is my rock. He is my firm foundation, and I can trust in Him completely." (Psalm 18:2)

Prayer

Heavenly Father,

Thank you for being my rock, my firm foundation. I surrender the brokenness in my home to you. Fill my family with your stability and strength. Guide us in finding our footing and building a solid foundation on your truth and love. Give us the assurance of your presence and security in the midst of the storm.

Forgive me for relying on my own strength or seeking stability in worldly things. Help me fully embrace the truth that you are my rock and let go of self-reliance.

Thank you for being my rock and providing stability and strength to my broken home. I trust in your promises and believe that you can bring restoration. Help me walk in the assurance of your presence, knowing that you are at work in my family.

In Jesus' name, I pray.

Amen.

Day 14: "I declare that God is my hope. He will give me hope for the future and fill my heart with His promises." (Jeremiah 29:11)

Prayer

Heavenly Father,

Thank you for being my hope and filling my heart with your promises. I surrender any feelings of hopelessness or despair to you. Help me embrace the truth that you have a purpose and plan for my life. Fill me with a deep understanding of the significance of your hope.

Father, I pray for your hope to be present in my life. Fill my heart with your promises and give me hope for the future, even in difficult circumstances. Help me trust your plans and walk in the assurance of your hope.

Forgive me for allowing doubt and fear to overshadow your hope. Help me fully embrace the truth that you are my hope and let go of doubt and fear.

Thank you for being my hope and filling my heart with your promises. I trust in your plans and believe you have a purpose for my life. Help me walk in the assurance of your hope, knowing you are at work in me.

In Jesus' name, I pray.

Amen.

Day 15: "I affirm that God is my protector. He will watch over me and keep me safe from harm." (Psalm 121:7)

Prayer

Heavenly Father,

Thank you for being my protector. I surrender the brokenness in my home to you. Fill my family with safety and security. Watch over us and shield us from harm. Give us the assurance of your presence and protection.

Forgive me for relying on my own strength or seeking protection in worldly things. Help me fully embrace the truth that you are my protector and let go of self-reliance.

Thank you for being my protector and keeping me safe. I trust in your promises and believe you can bring safety and restoration to my home. Help me walk in the assurance of your protection, knowing you are at work in my family.

In Jesus' name, I pray.

Amen.

Day 16: "I declare that God is my peace. He will give me peace that surpasses all understanding, even in the midst of chaos." (Philippians 4:7)

Prayer

Heavenly Father,

Thank you for being my peace in the midst of chaos. I surrender the brokenness in my home to you. Bring calm and tranquility to my family. Quiet the storms within us and replace them with your peace. Help me fully embrace the truth that you are my peace and let go of reliance on worldly things.

Thank you for giving me a peace that surpasses understanding. I trust in your promises and believe you can bring restoration to my home. Help me walk in the assurance of your peace, knowing you are at work in my family.

In Jesus' name, I pray.

Amen.

Day 17: "I affirm that God is my provider. He will supply all my needs according to His glorious riches in Christ Jesus." (Philippians 4:19)

Prayer

Heavenly Father,

Thank you for being my provider. I surrender the financial struggles and uncertainty in my family to you. Fill us with the understanding that you can meet all our needs. Provide for us in every area of our lives. Show us your faithfulness and guide us towards abundance. Help us let go of self-reliance and trust in your provision.

Thank you for being my provider and supplying all my needs. I trust in your promises and believe you can bring provision and restoration to my home. Help me walk in the assurance of your provision, knowing you are at work in my family.

In Jesus' name, I pray.

Amen.

Day 18: "I declare that God is my refuge. He is my safe place, and I can run to Him for shelter and protection." (Psalm 91:2)

Prayer

Heavenly Father,

You are our refuge, our safe place. We surrender the brokenness in our home to you. Fill us with the understanding that we can find safety and healing in your presence. Be our shelter from the storms of life, protecting us from harm and providing comfort. Help us let go of self-reliance and seek refuge in you.

Thank you for being our refuge and providing a safe place for us. We trust in your promises and believe you can bring healing and restoration to our home. Help us walk in the assurance of your refuge, knowing you are at work in our family.

In Jesus' name, we pray.

Amen.

Day 19: "I affirm that God is my strength. He will give me the strength to face each day with courage and confidence." (Isaiah 40:31)

Prayer

Heavenly Father,

You are my strength. I surrender the brokenness in my home to you. Fill us with the courage and confidence we need, knowing that you are with us. Strengthen each member of my family who is feeling weak or weary. Help us rely on your strength and let go of self-reliance. Thank you for being our strength and for bringing restoration to my family.

In Jesus' name, I pray.

Amen.

Day 20: "I declare that God is my helper. He will help me in times of trouble and give me the wisdom I need." (Psalm 46:1)

Prayer

Heavenly Father,

You are our helper. We surrender the brokenness in our home to you. Fill us with the understanding that we can rely on you for guidance and support. Be our guide and source of wisdom. Help us navigate through challenges and provide solutions. Give us the assurance that you are with us, helping us in times of trouble and giving us the wisdom we need.

Forgive us for relying on our own understanding or seeking help from worldly sources. Help us let go of self-reliance and depend on you.

Thank you for being our helper and providing us with wisdom. We trust in your promises and believe you can bring restoration to our home. Help us walk in the assurance of your help, knowing you are at work in our family.

In Jesus' name, we pray.

Amen.

Day 21: "I affirm that God is my comforter. He will bring me comfort and peace in times of sadness or loneliness." (2 Corinthians 1:3-4)

Prayer

Heavenly Father,

You are our comforter. I surrender the brokenness in broken homes to you. Fill them with your comfort and peace. Bring healing to their hearts and minds. Wrap your loving arms around them and provide the peace that surpasses all understanding. Give them the assurance that you are with them, bringing comfort and restoration to their brokenness.

Forgive us for seeking comfort in worldly things or relying on our own strength. Help us let go of self-reliance and depend on you.

Thank you for being our comforter and bringing us peace. We trust in your promises and believe you can bring comfort and restoration to broken homes. Help us walk in the assurance of your comfort, knowing you are at work in these families.

In Jesus' name, we pray.

Amen.

Day 22: "I declare that God is my joy. He will fill my heart with His joy, even in difficult times." (Psalm 16:11)

Prayer

Heavenly Father,

I come before you today, acknowledging that you are our joy. Thank you for the truth of Psalm 16:11, that in your presence there is fullness of joy and that you can fill our hearts with your joy, even in the midst of difficult times.

Lord, I surrender the brokenness in my home to you. I lay before you the pain, sadness, and despair that exist within my family. Help us to fully embrace the truth that you are our joy and that we can find true happiness and contentment in your presence. Fill us with a deep understanding of the significance of seeking your joy in our brokenness.

Father, I pray for your joy to be present in our home. Fill our hearts with your joy, even in the midst of our struggles. Bring laughter and happiness into our lives. Help us find solace and comfort in your presence. Give us the assurance that you are with us, bringing joy and restoration to our brokenness.

Thank you for being our joy and for filling our hearts with your joy. We trust in your promises and believe that you can bring joy and restoration to broken homes. Help us walk in the assurance of your joy, knowing that you are at work in our families.

In Jesus' name, I pray.

Amen.

Day 23: "I affirm that God is my guide. He will lead me on the right path and show me His perfect plan for my life." (Psalm 32:8)

Prayer

Heavenly Father,

I come before you today, acknowledging that you are our guide. Thank you for the truth of Psalm 32:8, that you will lead us on the right path and show us your perfect plan for our lives.

Lord, I surrender the brokenness in broken homes to you. I lay before you the pain, confusion, and uncertainty that exist within these families. Help them to fully embrace the truth that you are their guide and that they can trust in your leadership and direction. Fill them with a deep understanding of the significance of seeking your guidance in their lives.

Thank you for being our guide and for leading us on the right path. We trust in your promises and believe that you have a perfect plan for our lives. Help us walk in the assurance of your guidance, knowing that you are at work in these families.

In Jesus' name, I pray.

Amen.

Day 24: "I declare that God is my peace. He will calm my fears and anxieties and give me a sense of security." (John 14:27)

Prayer

Heavenly Father,

I come before you today, declaring that you are our peace. Thank you for the truth of John 14:27, that you will calm our fears and anxieties and give us a sense of security.

Lord, I surrender the brokenness in broken homes to you. I lay before you the fear, anxiety, and insecurity that exist within these families. Help them to fully embrace the truth that you are their peace and that they can find comfort and security in your presence. Fill them with a deep understanding of the significance of seeking your peace in their brokenness.

Thank you for being our peace and for calming our fears and anxieties. We trust in your promises and believe that you can bring peace and restoration to broken homes. Help us walk in the assurance of your peace, knowing that you are at work in these families.

In Jesus' name, I pray.

Amen.

Day 25: "I affirm that God is my strength. He will give me the strength to overcome any challenges or obstacles I may face." (Isaiah 40:29)

Prayer

Heavenly Father,

I come before you today, affirming that you are our strength. Thank you for the truth of Isaiah 40:29, that you will give us the strength to overcome any challenges or obstacles we may face.

Lord, I surrender the brokenness in broken homes to you. I lay before you the struggles, hardships, and difficulties that exist within these families. Help them to fully embrace the truth that you are their strength and that they can find the power to overcome in your presence. Fill them with a deep understanding of the significance of seeking your strength in their brokenness.

Thank you for being our strength and for giving us the power to overcome. We trust in your promises and believe that you can bring strength and restoration to broken homes. Help us walk in the assurance of your strength, knowing that you are at work in these families.

In Jesus' name, I pray.

Amen.

Day 26: "I declare that God is my comforter. He will bring me comfort and peace in times of sadness or grief." (2 Corinthians 1:3-4)

Prayer

Heavenly Father,

I come before you today, declaring that you are my comforter. Thank you for the truth of 2 Corinthians 1:3-4, that you will bring me comfort and peace in times of sadness or grief.

Lord, I surrender the brokenness in my home to you. I lay before you the sadness, grief, and pain that exist within my family. Help us to fully embrace the truth that you are our comforter and that we can find solace and peace in your presence. Fill us with a deep understanding of the significance of seeking your comfort in our brokenness.

Father, I pray for your comfort in being present in my home. Bring healing to our hearts and minds. Comfort us in our times of sadness and grief. Give us peace that surpasses all understanding. Help us to trust in your love and to find rest in your arms.

Thank you for being our comforter and for bringing us peace in times of sadness or grief. We trust in your promises and believe that you can bring comfort and restoration to broken homes. Help us walk in the assurance of your comfort, knowing that you are at work in our families.

In Jesus' name, I pray.

Amen.

Day 27: "I affirm that God is my rock. He is my firm foundation, and I can trust in Him completely." (Psalm 18:2)

Prayer

Heavenly Father,

I come before you today, affirming that you are our rock. Thank you for the truth of Psalm 18:2, that you are our firm foundation, and we can trust in you completely.

Lord, I surrender the brokenness in my home to you. I lay before you the pain, confusion, and instability that exist within my family. Help us to fully embrace the truth that you are our rock, our firm foundation, and that we can find stability and security in your presence. Fill us with a deep understanding of the significance of seeking you as our rock in our brokenness.

Father, I pray for your strength and stability to be present in my home. Be our firm foundation, holding us steady in the midst of the storms of life. Help us to trust in your unwavering love and faithfulness. Guide us in building our lives and family around the sold, rocking your truth.

Thank you for being our rock and our firm foundation. We trust in your promises and believe that you can bring stability and restoration to broken homes. Help us walk in the assurance of your presence, knowing that you are at work in our families.

In Jesus' name, I pray.

Amen.

Day 28: "I declare that God is my hope. He will give me hope for the future and fill my heart with His promises." (Jeremiah 29:11)

Prayer

Heavenly Father,

I come before you today, declaring that you are our hope. Thank you for the truth of Jeremiah 29:11, that you have plans to prosper us and give us hope for the future.

Lord, I surrender the brokenness in my home to you. I lay before you the pain, despair, and uncertainty that exist within my family. Help us to fully embrace the truth that you are our hope and that we can find strength and restoration in your promises. Fill us with a deep understanding of the significance of seeking you as our hope in our brokenness.

Father, I pray for your hope to be present in my home. Fill our hearts with your promises and your plans for our future. Give us the strength to endure the challenges and trials we face. Help us to trust in your faithfulness and to find hope in your love.

Thank you for being our hope and for filling our hearts with your promises. We trust in your plans and believe that you can bring restoration and hope to broken homes. Help us walk in the assurance of your hope, knowing that you are at work in our families.

In Jesus' name, I pray.

Amen.

Day 29: "I affirm that God is my protector. He will watch over me and keep me safe from harm." (Psalm 121:7)

Prayer

Heavenly Father,

I come before you today, affirming that you are our protector. Thank you for the truth of Psalm 121:7, that you will watch over us and keep us safe from harm.

Lord, I surrender the brokenness in my home to you. I lay before you the pain, chaos, and insecurity that exist within my family. Help us to fully embrace the truth that you are our protector and that we can find safety and security in your presence. Fill us with a deep understanding of the significance of seeking you as our protector in our brokenness.

Father, I pray for your protection and presence in my home. Watch over us and keep us safe from harm. Shield us from the attacks of the enemy and the dangers of this world. Protect us from the negative influences and destructive patterns that have caused brokenness in our family. Help us to trust in your divine protection and to find peace in your loving care.

Thank you for being our protector and for keeping us safe from harm. We trust in your promises and believe that you can bring protection and restoration to broken homes. Help us walk in the assurance of your presence, knowing that you are at work in our families.

In Jesus' name, I pray.

Amen.

Day 30: "I declare that God is my peace. He will give me peace that surpasses all understanding, even in the midst of chaos." (Philippians 4:7)

Prayer

Heavenly Father,

I come before you today, affirming that you are our peace. Thank you for the truth of Philippians 4:7, that you will give us a peace that surpasses all understanding, even in the midst of chaos.

Lord, I surrender the brokenness in my home to you. I lay before you the chaos, conflict, and unrest that exist within my family. Help us to fully embrace the truth that you are our peace and that we can find tranquility and harmony in your presence. Fill us with a deep understanding of the significance of seeking you as our peace in our brokenness.

Father, I pray for your peace to be present in my home. Bring calmness to our hearts and minds. Help us to let go of anger, bitterness, and resentment. Fill us with your love, forgiveness, and understanding. Guide us in seeking reconciliation and restoration within our family.

Thank you for being our peace and for giving us a peace that surpasses all understanding. We trust in your promises and believe that you can bring peace and restoration to broken homes. Help us walk in the assurance of your presence, knowing that you are at work in our families.

In Jesus' name, I pray.

Amen.

Day 31: "I affirm that God is my provider. He will supply all my needs according to His glorious riches in Christ Jesus." (Philippians 4:19)

Prayer

Heavenly Father,

I come before you today, affirming that you are our provider. Thank you for the truth of Philippians 4:19, that you will supply all our needs according to your glorious riches in Christ Jesus.

Lord, I surrender the brokenness in my home to you. I lay before you the financial struggles, lack, and uncertainty that exist within my family. Help us to fully embrace the truth that you are our provider and that we can find provision and abundance in your presence. Fill us with a deep understanding of the significance of seeking you as our provider in our brokenness.

Father, I pray for your provision to be present in my home. Supply all our needs according to your glorious riches in Christ Jesus. Help us to trust in your faithfulness and to find contentment in your provision. Guide us in making wise financial decisions and in stewarding the resources you have given us.

Thank you for being our provider and for supplying all our needs. We trust in your promises and believe that you can bring provision and restoration to broken homes. Help us walk in the assurance of your presence, knowing that you are at work in our families.

In Jesus' name, I pray.

Amen.

May these affirmations and declarations remind you that God is always with you, no matter the circumstances. He loves you deeply and will provide for you, comfort you, and guide you. Trust in His faithfulness and lean on His strength.

Amen.

CHARACTER CHECK

Day 1: Love

Affirmation: I am filled with the love of Christ, and I choose to love others unconditionally.

Declaration: "A new command I give you: Love one another. As I have loved you, so you must love one another." - John 13:34

Day 2: Compassion

Affirmation: I have a compassionate heart, and I show empathy and kindness to those in need.

Declaration: "Be kind and compassionate to one another, forgiving each other, just as in Christ God forgave you." - Ephesians 4:32

Day 3: Humility

Affirmation: I humble myself before God and others, putting their needs before my own.

Declaration: "Do nothing out of selfish ambition or vain conceit. Rather, in humility value others above yourselves." - Philippians 2:3

Day 4: Forgiveness

Affirmation: I forgive others as Christ has forgiven me, releasing any bitterness or resentment.

Declaration: "Bear with each other and forgive one another if any of you has a grievance against someone. Forgive as the Lord forgave you." - Colossians 3:13

Day 5: Patience

Affirmation: I am patient and understanding, trusting in God's timing and extending grace to others.

Declaration: "Be completely humble and gentle; be patient, bearing with one another in love." - Ephesians 4:2

Day 6: Kindness

Affirmation: I choose to be kind in my words and actions, showing the love of Christ to everyone I encounter.

Declaration: "Therefore, as God's chosen people, holy and dearly loved, clothe yourselves with compassion, kindness, humility, gentleness, and patience." - Colossians 3:12

Day 7: Integrity

Affirmation: I live with integrity, being honest and trustworthy in all areas of my life.

Declaration: "The integrity of the upright guides them, but the unfaithful are destroyed by their duplicity." - Proverbs 11:3

Day 8: Faithfulness

Affirmation: I am faithful in my commitments and relationships, reflecting the faithfulness of Christ.

Declaration: "Let love and faithfulness never leave you; bind them around your neck, write them on the tablet of your heart." - Proverbs 3:3

Day 9: Self-Control

Affirmation: I exercise self-control over my thoughts, words, and actions, allowing the Holy Spirit to guide me.

Declaration: "For the Spirit God gave us does not make us timid, but gives us power, love, and self-discipline." - 2 Timothy 1:7

Day 10: Joy

Affirmation: I choose joy in all circumstances, finding my strength and hope in Christ.

Declaration: "Rejoice in the Lord always. I will say it again: Rejoice!" - Philippians 4:4

Day 11: Gentleness

Affirmation: I am gentle in my interactions, treating others with kindness and respect.

Declaration: "Let your gentleness be evident to all. The Lord is near." - Philippians 4:5

Day 12: Peace

Affirmation: I have the peace of Christ that surpasses all understanding, and I bring peace to those around me.

Declaration: "And the peace of God, which transcends all understanding, will guard your hearts and your minds in Christ Jesus." - Philippians 4:7

Day 13: Generosity

Affirmation: I am generous with my time, resources, and love, reflecting the generosity of Christ.

Declaration: "Command them to do good, to be rich in good deeds, and to be generous and willing to share." - 1 Timothy 6:18

Day 14: Wisdom

Affirmation: I seek wisdom from God and make wise choices that align with His will.

Declaration: "If any of you lacks wisdom, you should ask God, who gives generously to all without finding fault, and it will be given to you." - James 1:5

Day 15: Servanthood

Affirmation: I have a servant's heart, willingly serving and helping others as Christ did.

Declaration: "For even the Son of Man did not come to be served, but to serve, and to give his life as a ransom for many." - Mark 10:45

Day 16: Gratitude

Affirmation: I am grateful for God's blessings and express gratitude in all circumstances.

Declaration: "Give thanks in all circumstances, for this is God's will for you in Christ Jesus." - 1 Thessalonians 5:18

Day 17: Trust

Affirmation: I trust in God's plan and His faithfulness, relying on Him in all areas of my life.

Declaration: "Trust in the Lord with all your heart and lean not on your own understanding; in all your ways submit to him, and he will make your paths straight." - Proverbs 3:5-6

Day 18: Courage

Affirmation: I have courage and boldness in my faith, stepping out in obedience to God's calling.

Declaration: "Be strong and courageous. Do not be afraid or terrified because of them, for the Lord your God goes with you; he will never leave you nor forsake you." - Deuteronomy 31:6

Day 19: Contentment

Affirmation: I am content in all circumstances, finding my satisfaction in Christ alone.

Declaration: "I know what it is to be in need, and I know what it is to have plenty. I have learned the secret of being content in any and every situation, whether well fed or hungry, whether living in plenty or in want." - Philippians 4:12

Day 20: Diligence

Affirmation: I am diligent and hardworking, using my talents and abilities for God's glory.

Declaration: "Whatever you do, work at it with all your heart, as working for the Lord, not for human masters." - Colossians 3:23

Day 21: Encouragement

Affirmation: I am an encourager, uplifting and inspiring others with my words and actions.

Declaration: "Therefore encourage one another and build each other up, just as, in fact, you are doing." - 1 Thessalonians 5:11

Day 22: Selflessness

Affirmation: I put the needs of others before my own, showing sacrificial love as Christ did.

Declaration: "Do nothing out of selfish ambition or vain conceit. Rather, in humility value others above yourselves." - Philippians 2:3

Day 23: Prayerfulness

Affirmation: I am Prayerful, seeking God's guidance and communing with Him daily.

Declaration: "Do not be anxious about anything, but in every situation, by Prayer and petition, with thanksgiving, present your requests to God." - Philippians 4:6

Day 24: Holiness

Affirmation: I pursue holiness and strive to live a life that is set apart for God's purposes.

Declaration: "But just as he who called you is holy, so be holy in all you do; for it is written: 'Be holy because I am holy.'" - 1 Peter 1:15-16

Day 25: Graciousness

Affirmation: I extend grace and forgiveness to others, just as God has shown me grace.

Declaration: "Let your conversation be always full of grace, seasoned with salt, so that you may know how to answer everyone." - Colossians 4:6

Day 26: Thankfulness

Affirmation: I am thankful for God's blessings and express gratitude in all circumstances.

Declaration: "Give thanks to the Lord, for he is good; his love endures forever." - Psalm 107:1

Day 27: Trust

Affirmation: I trust in God's plan and His faithfulness, relying on Him in all areas of my life.

Declaration: "Trust in the Lord with all your heart and lean not on your own understanding; in all your ways submit to him, and he will make your paths straight." - Proverbs 3:5-6

Day 28: Compassion

Affirmation: I have a compassionate heart, and I show empathy and kindness to those in need.

Declaration: "Be kind and compassionate to one another, forgiving each other, just as in Christ God forgave you." - Ephesians 4:32

Day 29: Resilience

Affirmation: I am resilient and persevere through challenges with God's strength.

Declaration: "I can do all this through him who gives me strength." - Philippians 4:13

Day 30: Compassionate Listening

Affirmation: I listen with compassion and seek to understand others.

Declaration: "My dear brothers and sisters, take note of this: Everyone should be quick to listen, slow to speak, and slow to become angry." - James 1:19

Day 31: Worship

Affirmation: I worship God with all my heart, mind, and soul.

Declaration: "Yet a time is coming and has now come when the true worshipers will worship the Father in the Spirit and in truth, for they are the kind of worshipers the Father seeks." - John 4:23

By affirming and declaring these character traits, we can align ourselves with the teachings of Christ and strive to live a life that reflects His love and grace. May these affirmations and declarations guide and inspire you on your journey of faith.

www.ingramcontent.com/pod-product-compliance
Lightning Source LLC
Chambersburg PA
CBHW051820150726
47998CB00001B/226